A READER'S GUIDE TO

CONTEMPORARY LITERARY THEORY

A READER'S GUIDE TO CONTEMPORARY LITERARY THEORY

RAMAN SELDEN

THE UNIVERSITY PRESS OF KENTUCKY

Published by the University Press of Kentucky,
scholarly publisher for the Commonwealth,
serving Bellarmine College, Berea College, Centre
College of Kentucky, Eastern Kentucky University,
The Filson Club, Georgetown College, Kentucky
Historical Society, Kentucky State University,
Morehead State University, Murray State University,
Northern Kentucky University, Transylvania University,
University of Kentucky, University of Louisville,
and Western Kentucky University.

Editorial and Sales Offices: Lexington, Kentucky 40506-0024

Library of Congress Cataloging in Publication Data
Selden, Raman.
A reader's guide to contemporary literary theory.
Includes bibliographies and index.
1. Criticism—History—20th century. I. Title.
PN94.S45 1985 801'.95'0904 85-5353
ISBN 0-8131-1560-4
ISBN 0-8131-0167-0 (pbk.)

CONTENTS

INTRODUCTION

Until recently ordinary readers of literature and even professional literary critics had no reason to trouble themselves about developments in literary theory. Theory seemed a rather rarefied specialism which concerned a few individuals in literature departments who were, in effect, philosophers pretending to be literary critics. Discussions about literature, whether book reviews in the press, or in arts magazines on radio and television, were addressed to the ordinary reader. Most critics assumed, like Dr Johnson, that great literature was universal and expressed general truths about human life, and that therefore readers required no special knowledge or language. Critics talked comfortable good sense about the writer's personal experience, the social and historical background of the work, the human interest, imaginative 'genius', and poetic beauty of great literature. In other words, criticism spoke about literature without disturbing our picture of the world or of ourselves as readers. Then, at the end of the 1960s, things began to change.

During the past fifteen years or so students of literature have been troubled by a seemingly endless series of challenges to the consensus of common sense. To make things worse, most of the strange noises came from abroad. The English are particularly adept at shrugging off intellectual heavyweights from the Continent. We often complain that German theorists are too unwieldy and that the French are incorrigible rationalists. In this way we bolster up our cultural chauvinism and keep the foreign invaders at bay.

'Structuralism' hit the headlines when Colin MacCabe failed to obtain a tenured appointment at Cambridge University in 1980. The protests of the structuralists and their allies at Cambridge alerted the quality papers to the existence of an intruder in the bed of Dr Leavis's *alma mater*. The *Times Literary Supplement* duly published a special number on the scandal and its intellectual background. Most general readers of the newspaper accounts must have emerged more confused about 'structuralism' than they were before the 'MacCabe affair' gave the theorists a chance to explain themselves to the public. To be told that there was a touch of *Marxism* about MacCabe's structuralism, that his approach to structuralism was really a *post-structuralist* critique of structuralism, and that the main influence on his work was the *psychoanalytic* structuralism of the French philosopher Jacques Lacan, only confirmed ingrained prejudices.

I decided to undertake the daunting task of writing a reader's guide to this subject mainly because I believe that the questions raised by modern literary theory are important enough to justify the effort of clarification. Many readers now feel that the usual contemptuous dismissal of theory will not do. They would like to know exactly what they are being asked to reject. Inevitably any attempt to put together a brief summation of complex and contentious concepts will drain much of the blood from the body of a theory, and leave it even more vulnerable to the teeth of sceptics. However, I have assumed that the reader is *interested* and *curious* about the subject, and therefore ready to accept lightly seasoned fare as a preparation for the more authentic and pungent flavours of the original theories. I must acknowledge that I have perpetrated some gross over-simplifications in an attempt to say much in little. I hope that the reader will not be seriously misled by such unavoidable compressions and sweeping generalisations. I have provided at the end of each section graded 'further reading' to enable the reader to follow up particular approaches at various levels of difficulty.

Why should we trouble ourselves about literary theory? Can't we simply wait for the fuss to die down? The signs are that the graft of theory has taken rather well, and may remain intact for the foreseeable future. New journals have been launched, new courses established, and conferences devoted to theoretical questions. We should not be surprised if this new critical self-awareness manifests itself in the new generation of school teachers of literature. How does all this affect our experience and understanding of reading and writing? First, an emphasis on theory tends to undermine reading as an *innocent* activity. If we ask ourselves questions about the construction of meaning in fiction or the presence of ideology in poetry, we can no longer naively accept the 'realism' of a novel or the 'sincerity' of a poem. Some readers may cherish their illusions and mourn the loss of innocence, but, if they are serious readers, they cannot ignore the deeper issues raised by the major literary theorists in recent years. Secondly, far from having a sterile effect on our reading, new ways of seeing literature can revitalise our engagement with texts. Of course, if one has no desire to reflect upon one's reading, literary criticism of any sort will have little to offer. Alternatively, readers may believe that theories and concepts will only deaden the spontaneity of their response to literary works. They may forget that 'spontaneous' discourse about literature is unconsciously dependent on the theorising of older generations. Their talk of 'feeling', 'imagination', 'genius', 'sincerity', and 'reality' is full of dead theory which is sanctified by time and has become part of the language of common sense. If we are to be adventurous and exploratory in our reading of literature, we must also be adventurous in our thinking about literature.

One can think of the various literary theories as raising different questions about literature. Theories may ask questions from the point of view of the writer, of the work, of the reader, or of what we usually call 'reality'. Of course, no theorist will admit to being partial and will usually attempt to take account of the other points of view within the framework of the chosen approach. The following diagram of linguistic communication, devised by Roman Jakobson, helps to distinguish the various viewpoints:

CONTEXT
ADDRESSER → MESSAGE → ADDRESSEE
CONTACT
CODE

An addresser sends a message to an addressee; the message uses a code (usually a language familiar to both addresser and addressee); the message has a context (or 'referent') and is transmitted through a contact (a medium, such as live speech, a telephone, or writing). We may omit the 'contact' for the purpose of discussing literature; it is not of special interest to literary theorists, since contact is usually through the printed word (except in drama). We may restate the diagram thus:

	CONTEXT	
WRITER	WRITING	READER
	CODE	

Jakobson attaches a linguistic function to each element in the diagram as follows:

	REFERENTIAL	
EMOTIVE	POETIC	CONNOTATIVE
	METALINGUISTIC	

If we adopt the addresser's viewpoint, we draw attention to the emotive use of language; if we focus on the context, we isolate the referential use of language, etc. Literary theories, too, tend to place an emphasis upon one function rather than another. Taking the main theories we are about to discuss, we might place them diagrammatically as follows:

	MARXIST	
ROMANTIC	FORMALISTIC	READER-
	STRUCTURALIST	ORIENTED

Romantic theories emphasise the *writer's* mind and life; 'reader-criticism' (phenomenological criticism) centres itself on the *reader's* experience; formalist theories concentrate on the nature of *writing* itself in isolation; Marxist criticism regards the social and historical *context* as fundamental; and structuralist poetics draws attention to the *codes* we used to construct meaning. At their best none of the approaches totally ignores the other dimensions of literary communication. For example, in Marxist criticism, the writer, the audience, and the text are all included within a generally sociological perspective. Feminist criticism cannot be given a place in our diagram because it is not an 'approach' in the sense that applies to the other kinds of theory. Feminist criticism attempts a global re-interpretation of all approaches from a distinctly revolutionary standpoint.

I have not tried to give a comprehensive picture of modern

critical theory, but rather a guide to the most challenging and prominent trends. I have omitted, for example, myth criticism, which has a long and various history, and includes the work of such writers as Gilbert Murray, James Frazer, Maud Bodkin, Carl Jung, and Northrop Frye. It seemed to me that myth criticism has not entered the main stream of academic or popular culture, and has not challenged received ideas as vigorously as the theories we will examine.

CHAPTER ONE

RUSSIAN FORMALISM

Students of literature brought up in the tradition of Anglo-American New Criticism with its emphasis on 'practical criticism' and the organic unity of the text might expect to feel at home with Russian Formalism. Both kinds of criticism aim to explore what is specifically *literary* in texts, and both reject the limp spirituality of late Romantic poetics in favour of a detailed and empirical approach to reading. That being said, it must be admitted that the Russian Formalists were much more interested in 'method', much more concerned to establish a 'scientific' basis for the theory of literature. The New Critics combined attention to the specific verbal ordering of texts with an emphasis on the *non-conceptual* nature of literary meaning: a poem's complexity embodied a subtle response to life, which could not be reduced to logical statements or paraphrases. Their approach, despite the emphasis on close reading of texts, remained fundamentally humanistic. For example, Cleanth Brooks concluded his account by arguing that like all 'great poetry' the poem embodies 'honesty and insight and whole-mindedness'. The first Russian Formalists on the other hand Brooks concluded his account by arguing that like all 'great poetry' the poem embodies 'honesty and insight and whole-mindedness'. The first Russian Formalists on the other hand considered that human 'content' (emotions, ideas, and 'reality' in general) possessed no literary significance in itself, but merely provided a context for the functioning of literary 'devices'. As we shall see, this sharp division of form and content was modified by the later Formalists, but it remains true that the Formalists avoided the New Critics' tendency to endow aesthetic form with moral and cultural significance. They aimed rather to outline models and hypotheses (in a scientific spirit) to explain how aesthetic effects are produced by literary devices, and how the 'literary' is distinguished from and related to the 'extra-literary'. While the New Critics regarded literature as a form of human understanding, the Formalists thought of it as a special use of language.

The historical development of Formalism

Formalist studies were well established before the 1917 Revolution—in the Moscow Linguistic Circle, founded 1915, and in Opojaz (the letters stand for 'The Society for the Study of Poetic Language'), started in 1916. The leading figure of the former group was Roman Jakobson, who later helped to found the Prague Linguistic Circle in 1926. Viktor Shklovsky and Boris Eikenbaum were prominent in the latter group. The initial impetus was provided by the Futurists whose artistic efforts before the First World War were directed against 'decadent' bourgeois culture and especially against the anguished soul-searching of the Symbolist movement in poetry and the visual arts. They derided the mystical posturing of poets such as Briusov who insisted that the poet was 'the guardian of the mystery'. In place of the 'absolute', Mayakovsky, the extrovert Futurist poet, offered the noisy materialism of the machine age as the home of poetry. However, it should be noted that the Futurists were as opposed to Realism as the Symbolists had been: their slogan of the 'self-sufficient word' placed a stress on the self-contained sound patterning of words as distinct from their ability to refer to things. The Futurists threw themselves behind the Revolution and emphasised the artist's role as (proletarian) producer of crafted objects. Dmitriev declared that 'the artist is now simply a constructor and technician, a leader and foreman'. The Constructivists took these arguments to their logical extreme and entered actual factories to put into practice their theories of 'production art'.

From this background the Formalists set about producing a theory of literature concerned with the writer's *technical* prowess and *craft* skill. They avoided the proletarian rhetoric of the poets and artists, but they retained a somewhat mechanistic view of the literary process. Shklovsky was as vigorously materialistic in his attitudes as Mayakovsky. The former's famous definition of literature as 'the sum total of all stylistic devices employed in it' sums up well this early phase of formalism.

At first, the Formalists' work was allowed to develop freely in a USSR preoccupied with civil war, foreign interventions, and the ensuing social and economic distress. However, Trotsky's sophisticated criticisms of formalism in *Literature and Revolution* (1924) ushered in a new defensive phase, culminating in the Jakobson/Tynyanov theses (1928). Some regard the later developments as signalling the defeat of pure formalism and a capitulation to the Communist 'social command'. I would argue that, before official disapproval brought an end to the movement in about 1930, the need to take account of the sociological dimension produced some of the best work of the period, especially in the writings of the 'Bakhtin School' which combined formalist and Marxist traditions in fruitful ways that anticipated later developments. The more structuralist type of formalism, initiated by Jakobson and Tynyanov, was continued in Czech formalism (notably by the Prague Linguistic Circle), until Nazism brought it to an end. Some of this group, including René Wellek and Roman Jakobson, emigrated to the United States where they profoundly influenced the development of New Criticism during the 1940s and 1950s.

Art as device

The Formalists' technical focus led them to treat literature as a special use of language which achieves its distinctness by deviating from and distorting 'practical' language. Practical language is used for acts of communication, while literary language has no practical function at all and simply makes us *see* differently. One might apply this fairly easily to a writer such as Gerard Manley Hopkins, whose language is 'difficult' in a way which draws attention to itself as 'literary'. The earlier Formalists tended to identify 'literariness' with poeticalness. It is easy to show that there is no intrinsically literary language. Opening Hardy's *Under the Greenwood Tree* at random, I read the exchange '"How long will you be?" "Not long. Do wait and talk to me."' There is absolutely no linguistic reason to regard the words as 'literary'. We read them as literary rather than as an act of communication only because we read them in what we take to be a literary work. As we shall see, Tynyanov and others developed a more dynamic view of 'literariness' which avoids this problem.

What distinguishes literature from 'practical' language is its *constructed* quality. Poetry was treated by the Formalists as the quintessentially literary use of language: it is 'speech organised in its entire phonic texture'. Its most important constructive factor is rhythm. Consider a line from Donne's 'A Nocturnal upon St Lucies Day', stanza 2:

For I am every dead thing

A Formalist analysis would draw attention to an underlying iambic impulse (laid down in the equivalent line in the first stanza: 'The Sunne is spent, and now his flasks'). In the line from stanza 2, our anticipation is frustrated by a dropped syllable between 'dead' and 'thing'; we perceive a deviation from the norm, and this is what produces aesthetic significance. A Formalist would also note finer differences of rhythm produced by syntactical differences between the two lines (for example, the first has a strong caesura, the second none). Poetry exercises a controlled violence upon practical language, which is thereby deformed in order to compel our attention to its constructed nature.

The earlier phase of Formalism was dominated by Viktor Shklovsky, whose theorising, influenced by the Futurists, was lively and iconoclastic. While the Symbolists had viewed poetry as the expression of the Infinite or some unseen reality, Shklovsky adopted a down-to-earth approach, seeking to define the techniques which writers use to produce specific effects.

Shklovsky called one of his most attractive concepts 'defamiliarisation' (*ostranenie*: 'making strange'). He argued that we can never retain the freshness of our perceptions of objects; the demands of 'normal' existence require that they must become to a great extent 'automatised' (a later term). That Wordsworthian innocent vision through which Nature retains 'the glory and the freshness of a dream' is not the normal state of human consciousness. It is the special task of art to give us back the awareness of things which have become habitual objects of our everyday awareness. It must be stressed that the Formalists, unlike the Romantic poets, were not so much interested in the perceptions themselves as in the nature of the devices which produce the effect of 'defamiliarisation'. In 'Art as Technique' (1917), Shklovsky makes this clear:

> The purpose of art is to impart the sensation of things as they are perceived, and not as they are known. The technique of art is to make objects 'unfamiliar', to make forms difficult, to increase the difficulty and length of perception, because the process of perception is an aesthetic end in itself and must be prolonged. *Art is a way of experiencing the artfulness of an object; the object is not important.* (Shklovsky's emphasis)

The Formalists were fond of citing two English eighteenth-century writers, Laurence Sterne and Jonathan Swift. Tomashevsky shows how devices of defamiliarisation are used in *Gulliver's Travels*:

> In order to present a satirical picture of the European social-political order, Gulliver... tells his master (a horse) about the customs of the ruling class in human society. Compelled to tell everything with the utmost accuracy, he removes the shell of euphemistic phrases and fictitious traditions which justify such things as war, class strife, parliamentary intrigue and so on. Stripped of their verbal justification and thus defamiliarised, these topics emerge in all their horror. Thus criticism of the political system—nonliterary material—is artistically motivated and fully involved in the narrative.

At first this account seems to stress the content of the new perception itself ('horror' at 'war' and 'class strife'). But in fact, what interests Tomashevsky is the artistic transformation of 'nonliterary material'. Defamiliarisation changes our response to the world but only by submitting our habitual perceptions to the processes of literary form.

In his monograph on Sterne's *Tristram Shandy*, Shklovsky draws attention to the ways in which familiar actions are defamiliarised by being slowed down, drawn out or interrupted. This technique of delaying and protracting actions makes us attend to them, so that familiar sights and movements cease to be perceived automatically and are thus 'defamiliarised'. Mr Shandy, lying despondently on his bed after hearing of his son

Tristram's broken nose, might have been described conventionally ('he lay mournfully upon his bed'), but Sterne chose to defamiliarise Mr Shandy's posture:

> **The palm of his right hand, as he fell upon the bed, receiving his forehead, and covering the greatest part of both his eyes, gently sunk down with his head (his elbow giving way backwards) till his nose touch'd the quilt; – his left arm hung insensible over the side of the bed, his knuckles reclining upon the handle of the chamber pot...**

The example is interesting in showing how often defamiliarisation affects not a perception as such but merely the presentation of a perception. By slowing down the description of Mr Shandy's posture, Sterne gives us no new insight into grief, no new perception of a familiar posture, but only a heightened verbal presentation. It is Sterne's very lack of concern with perception in the non-literary sense which seems to attract Shklovsky's admiration. This emphasis on the actual process of presentation is called 'laying bare' one's technique. Many readers find Sterne's novel irritating for its continual references to its own novelistic structure, but 'laying bare' its own devices is, in Shklovsky's view, the most essentially *literary* thing a novel can do.

'Defamiliarisation' and 'laying bare' are notions which directly influenced Bertold Brecht's famous 'alienation effect'. The classical ideal that art should *conceal* its own processes (*ars celare artem*) was directly challenged by the Formalists and by Brecht. For literature to present itself as a seamless unity of discourse and as a natural representation of reality would be deceitful and, for Brecht, politically regressive. For example, in a Brechtian production a male character may be played by an actress in order to destroy the naturalness and familiarity of the role and by defamiliarising the role to make the audience attend to its specific maleness. The possible political uses of the device were not foreseen by the Formalists, since their concerns were purely technical.

Narrative

Greek tragedians drew upon traditional stories which consisted of a series of incidents. In section 6 of the *Poetics*, Aristotle defines 'plot' ('mythos') as the 'arrangement of the incidents'. A 'plot' is clearly distinguished from a story upon which a plot may be based. A plot is the artful disposition of the incidents which make up a story. A Greek tragedy usually starts with a 'flash-back', a recapitulation of the incidents of the story which occurred prior to those which were selected for the plot. In Virgil's *Aeneid* and in Milton's *Paradise Lost*, the reader is plunged *in medias res* ('into the middle of things'), and earlier incidents in the story are introduced artfully at various stages in the plot, often in the form of retrospective narration: Aeneas narrates the Fall of Troy to Dido in Carthage, and Raphael relates the War in Heaven to Adam and Eve in Paradise.

The distinction between 'story' and 'plot' is given a prominent place in the Russian Formalists' theory of narrative. They stress that only 'plot' (*sjuzet*) is strictly literary, while 'story' (*fabula*) is merely raw material awaiting the organising hand of the writer. However, as Shklovsky's essay on Sterne reveals, the Formalists had a more revolutionary concept of plot than Aristotle. The plot of *Tristram Shandy* is not merely the arrangement of story-incidents but also all the 'devices' used to interrupt and delay the narration. Digressions, typographical games, displacement of parts of the book (preface, dedication, etc.), and extended descriptions, are all devices for making us attend to the novel's form. In a sense, 'plot', in this instance, is actually the violation of the expected formal arrangements of incidents. By frustrating familiar plot arrangement, Sterne draws attention to plotting itself as a literary object. In this way, Shklovsky is not at all Aristotelian. In the end, a carefully ordered Aristotelian 'plot' should give us the essential and familiar truths of human life; it should be plausible and have a certain inevitability. The Formalists, on the other hand, often linked theory of plot with the notion of defamiliarisation: the plot *prevents* us from regarding the incidents as typical and familiar.

Motivation

Boris Tomashevsky called the smallest unit of plot a 'motif', which we may understand as a single statement or action. He makes a distinction between 'bound' and 'free' motifs. A bound motif is one which is required by the story, while a 'free' motif is inessential from the point of view of the story. However, from the literary point of view, the 'free' motifs are potentially the focus of art. For example, the device of having Raphael relate the War in Heaven is a 'free' motif, because it is not part of the story in question. However, it is formally *more* important than the narration of the War itself, because it enables Milton to insert the narration artistically into his overall plot.

This approach reverses the traditional subordination of formal devices to 'content'. The Formalists rather perversely seem to regard a poem's ideas, themes, and references to 'reality' as merely the external excuse the writer required to justify the use of formal devices. They called this dependence on external, non-literary assumptions 'motivation'. According to Shklovsky, *Tristram Shandy* is remarkable for being totally without 'motivation'; the novel is entirely made up of formal devices which are 'bared'.

The most familiar type of 'motivation' is what we usually call 'realism'. No matter how formally constructed a work may be, we still often expect it to give us the illusion of the 'real'. We expect literature to be 'life-like', and may be irritated by characters or descriptions which fail to match our common-sense expectations of what the real world is like. 'A man in love wouldn't behave like that' and 'people of that class wouldn't talk like that' are the kind of remarks we might make when we notice a failure of realistic motivation. On the other hand, as Tomashevsky pointed out, we become accustomed to all kinds of absurdities and improbabilities once we learn to accept a new set of conventions. We fail to notice the improbable way in which heroes are always rescued just before they are about to be killed by the villains in adventure stories.

The theme of 'motivation' turned out to be important in a great deal of subsequent literary theory. Jonathan Culler summed up the general theme neatly when he wrote: 'To assimilate or interpret something is to bring it within the modes of order which culture makes available, and this is usually done by talking about it in a mode of discourse which a culture takes as natural.' Human beings are endlessly inventive in finding ways of making sense of the most random or chaotic utterances or inscriptions. We refuse to allow a text to remain alien and outside our frames of reference; we insist on 'naturalising' it, and effacing its textuality. When faced with a page of apparently random images, we prefer to naturalise it by attributing the images to a disordered mind or by regarding it as a reflection of a disordered world, rather than to accept its disorder as strange and inexplicable. The Formalists anticipated structuralist and post-structuralist thought by attending to those features of texts which resist the relentless process of naturalisation. Shklovsky refused to reduce the bizarre disorder of *Tristram Shandy* to an expression of Tristram's quirky mind, and instead drew attention to the novel's insistent literariness which resists naturalisation (and yet cannot finally avoid it).

The dominant

It gradually became apparent that literary devices were not fixed pieces that could be moved at will in the literary game. Their value and meaning changed with time and also with context. With this realisation, 'device' gave way to 'function' as the leading concept. The effect of this shift was far-reaching. Formalists were no longer plagued by an unresolved rejection of 'content', but were able to internalise the central principle of 'defamiliarisation'; that is to say, instead of having to talk about literature defamiliarising reality, they could begin to refer to the defamiliarising of literature itself. Elements *within* a work may become 'automatised' or may have a positive aesthetic function. The same device may have different aesthetic functions in different works or may become totally automatised. For example, archaisms and Latinate word order may have an 'elevating' function in an epic poem, or an ironic function in a satire, or even become totally automatised as general 'poetic diction'. In the last case, the device is not 'perceived' by the reader as a functional element, and is effaced in the same way as ordinary perceptions become automatised and taken for granted. Literary works are seen as *dynamic systems* in which elements are structured in relations of foreground and background. If a particular element is 'effaced' (perhaps archaic diction), other elements will come into play as dominant (perhaps plot or rhythm) in the work's system. Writing in 1935, Jakobson regarded 'the dominant' as an important late Formalist concept, and defined it as 'the focusing component of a work of art: it rules, determines, and transforms the remaining components'. He rightly stresses the non-mechanistic aspect of this view of artistic structure. The dominant provides the work with its focus of crystallisation and facilitates its unity or *gestalt* (total order). The very notion of defamiliarisation implied *change* and historical development. Rather than look for eternal verities which bind all great literature into a single canon, the Formalists were disposed to see the history of literature as one of permanent revolution. Each new development is an attempt to repulse the dead hand of familiarity and habitual response. This dynamic notion of the dominant also provided the Formalists with a useful way of explaining literary history. Poetic forms change and develop not at random but as a result of a 'shifting dominant': there is a continuing shift in the mutual relationships among the various elements in a poetic system. Jakobson added the interesting idea that the poetics of particular periods may be governed by a 'dominant' which derives from a non-literary system. The dominant of Renaissance poetry was derived from the visual arts; Romantic poetry oriented itself towards music; and Realism's dominant is verbal art. But whatever the dominant may be, it organises the other elements in the individual work, relegating to the background of aesthetic attention elements which in works of earlier periods might have been 'foregrounded' as dominant. What changes is not so much the elements of the system (syntax, rhythm, plot, diction, etc.) but the *function* of particular elements or groups of elements. When Pope wrote the following lines satirising the antiquarian, he could rely on the dominance of the values of prose clarity to help him achieve his purpose:

> But who is he, in closet close y-pent,
> Of sober face, with learned dust besprent?
> Right well mine eyes arede the myster wight,
> On parchment scraps y-fed, and Wormius hight.

The Chaucerian diction and archaic word-order are immediately treated by the reader as comically pedantic. In an earlier period Spenser was able to hark back to Chaucer's style without calling up the satiric note. The shifting dominant not only operates within particular texts but within particular literary periods.

The Bakhtin School

In the later period of Formalism, the so-called Bakhtin School combined Formalism and Marxism in a fruitful way. The authorship of several key works of the group is disputed and we are compelled simply to refer to the names which appear on the original title pages—Mikhail Bakhtin, Pavel Medvedev, and Valentin Voloshinov. The School remained formalist in its concern for the linguistic structure of literary works, but was deeply influenced by Marxism in its belief that language could not be separated from ideology. This intimate connection between language and ideology immediately drew literature into the social and economic sphere, the homeland of ideology. This approach departs from classical Marxist assumptions about ideology by refusing to treat it as a purely mental phenomenon which arises as a reflex of a material (real) socio-economic substructure. Ideology is not separable from its medium—language. As Voloshinov put it, 'consciousness itself can arise and become a viable fact only in the material embodiment of signs'. Language, a socially-constructed sign-system, is itself a material reality.

The Bakhtin School was not interested in abstract linguistics of the kind which later formed the basis of structuralism. They were concerned with language or discourse as a social phenomenon. Voloshinov's central insight was that 'words' are active, dynamic social signs, capable of taking on different meanings and connotations for different social classes in different social and historical situations. He attacked those linguists (including Saussure) who treated language as a dead, neutral, and static object of investigation. He rejected the whole notion of 'The isolated, finished, monologic utterance, divorced from its verbal and actual context and standing open not to any possible sort of active response but to passive understanding'. The Russian *slovo* may be translated 'word' but is used by the

Bakhtin School with a strongly social flavour (nearer to 'utterance' or 'discourse'). Verbal signs are the arena of continuous class struggle: the ruling class will always try to narrow the meaning of words and to make social signs 'uni-accentual', but in times of social unrest the vitality and basic 'multi-accentuality' of linguistic signs becomes apparent as various class interests clash and intersect upon the ground of language.

It was Mikhail Bakhtin who developed the implications of this dynamic view of language for literary texts. However, he did not, as one might have expected, treat literature as a direct reflection of social forces, but retained a formalist concern with literary structure, showing how the dynamic and active nature of language was given expression in certain literary traditions. He stressed not the way texts reflect society or class interests, but rather the way language is made to disrupt authority and liberate alternative voices. A libertarian language is entirely appropriate in describing Bakhtin's approach, which is very much a celebration of those writers whose work permits the freest play of different value systems and whose authority is not imposed upon the alternatives. Bakhtin is profoundly un-Stalinist! His classic work is *Problems of Dostoevsky's Poetics* (1929), in which he developed a bold contrast between the novels of Tolstoy and those of Dostoevsky. In the former, the various voices we hear are strictly subordinated to the author's controlling purpose: there is only one truth—the author's. In contrast to this 'monologic' type of novel, Dostoevsky developed a new 'polyphonic' (or dialogic) form, in which no attempt is made to orchestrate or unify the various points of view expressed in the various characters. The consciousness of the various characters does not merge with the author's nor do they become subordinated to the author's viewpoint, but they retain an integrity and independence; they are 'not only objects of the author's word, but subjects of their own directly significant word as well'. In this book and in his later one on Rabelais, Bakhtin explores the liberating and often subversive use of various dialogue forms in classical, medieval and Renaissance culture.

Bakhtin's discussion of 'carnival' has important applications both to particular texts and to the history of literary genres. The festivities associated with carnival are collective and popular;

hierarchies are turned on their heads (fools become wise, kings become beggars); opposites are mingled (fact and fantasy, heaven and hell); the sacred is profaned. The 'jolly relativity' of all things is proclaimed. Everything authoritative, rigid or serious is subverted, loosened and mocked. This essentially popular and libertarian social phenomenon has a formative influence on literature of various periods, but becomes especially dominant in the Renaissance. 'Carnivalisation' is the term Bakhtin uses to describe the shaping effect of carnival on literary genres. The earliest carnivalised literary forms are the Socratic dialogue and the Menippean satire. The former is in its origins close to the immediacy of oral dialogue, in which the discovery of truth is conceived as an unfolding exchange of views rather than as an authoritative monologue. The Socratic dialogues come down to us in the sophisticated literary forms devised by Plato. Some of the 'jolly relativity' of carnival survives in the written works, but there is also, in Bakhtin's view, some dilution of that collective quality of enquiry in which points of view collide without a strict hierarchy of voices being established by the 'author'. In the last Platonic dialogues, argues Bakhtin, the later image of Socrates as the 'teacher' begins to emerge and to replace the carnivalistic image of Socrates as the grotesque hen-pecked provoker of argument, who was midwife rather than author of truth.

In Menippean satire, the three planes of Heaven (Olympus), the Underworld, and Earth are all treated to the logic of carnival. For example, in the underworld earthly inequalities are dissolved; emperors lose their crowns and meet on equal terms with beggars. Dostoevsky brings together the various traditions of carnivalised literature. The 'fantastic tale' *Bobok* (1873) is almost pure Menippean satire. A scene in a cemetery culminates in a weird account of the brief 'life outside life' of the dead in the grave. Before losing their earthly consciousness completely, the dead enjoy a period of a few months when they are released from all the obligations and laws of normal existence and are able to reveal themselves with a stark and unlimited freedom. Baron Klinevich, 'king' of the corpses, declares 'I just want everyone to tell the truth . . . On earth it is impossible to live without lying, because life and lie are synonyms; but here we will tell the truth just for fun.' This contains the seed of the 'polyphonic' novel, in which voices are set free to speak subversively or shockingly, but without the author stepping between character and reader.

Bakhtin raises a number of themes developed by later theorists. Both Romantics and Formalists regarded texts as organic unities, as integrated structures in which all loose ends are finally gathered up into aesthetic unity by the reader. Bakhtin's emphasis on carnival breaks up this unquestioned organicism and promotes the idea that major literary works may be multi-levelled and resistant to unification. This leaves the author in a much less dominant position in relation to his writings. The notion of individual identity is left problematic: character is elusive, insubstantial, and quirky. This anticipates a major concern of recent psychoanalytic criticism, although one should not exaggerate this, or forget that Bakhtin still retains a firm sense of the writer's controlling artistry. His work does not imply the radical questioning of the role of author which arises in the work of Roland Barthes and other structuralists. However, Bakhtin does resemble Barthes in his 'privileging' of the polyphonic novel. Both critics prefer liberty and pleasure to authority and decorum. There is a tendency among recent critics to treat polyphonic and other kinds of 'plural' text as normative rather than as eccentric; that is, they treat them as more truly literary than more univocal (monologic) kinds of writing. This may appeal to modern readers brought up on Joyce and Beckett, but we must also recognise that both Bakhtin and Barthes are indicating *preferences* which arise from their own social and ideological predispositions. Nevertheless, it remains true that, asserting the openness and instability of literary texts, Bakhtin initiated a fruitful line of development.

The aesthetic function

We have already discussed the shift from Shklovsky's notion of the text as a heap of devices to Tynyanov's of the text as a functioning system. The high point of this 'structural' phase was the series of statements known as the Jakobson-Tynyanov theses (1928). The theses reject a mechanical formalism and attempt to reach beyond a narrowly literary perspective by trying to define the relationship between the literary 'series' (system) and other 'historical series'. The way in which the literary system develops historically cannot be understood, they argue, without understanding the way in which other systems impinge on it and partly determine its evolutionary path. On the other hand, they insist, we must attend to the 'immanent laws' of the literary system itself if we are to understand correctly the correlation of the systems. Despite the forbiddingly abstract nature of these formulations, they represent an impressive programme for research, and one which is yet to be undertaken.

The Prague Linguistic Circle, founded in 1926, continued and developed the 'structural' approach. Mukařovský, for example, underlined the folly of excluding extra-literary factors from critical analysis. Taking over Tynyanov's dynamic view of aesthetic structures, he placed great emphasis on the dynamic tension between literature and society in the artistic product. Mukařovský's most powerful argument concerned the 'aesthetic function', which proves to be an ever-shifting boundary and not a watertight category. The same object can possess several functions: a church may be both a place of worship and a work of art; a stone may be a door-stop, a missile, building material, and an object of artistic appreciation. Fashions are especially complex signs and may possess social, political, erotic and aesthetic functions. The same variability of function can be seen in literary products. A political speech, a biography, a letter, and a piece of propaganda, may or may not possess aesthetic value in different societies and periods. The circumference of the sphere of 'art' is always changing, and always dynamically related to the structure of society.

Mukařovsky's insight has been taken up recently by Marxist critics to establish the social bearings of art and literature. We can never talk about 'literature' as if it were a fixed canon of works, a specific set of devices, or an unchanging body of forms and genres. To endow an object or artifact with the dignity of aesthetic value is a *social* act, ultimately inseparable from prevailing ideologies. Modern social changes have resulted in certain artifacts, which once had mainly non-aesthetic functions, being regarded as primarily art-objects. The religious function of icons, the domestic function of Greek vases, and the military function of breast-plates, have been subordinated in modern times to a primarily aesthetic function. What people choose to regard as 'serious' art or 'high' culture is also subject to changing values. Jazz, for example, once merely music for brothels and bars, has become serious art, although its 'low' social origins still give rise to conflicting evaluations. From this perspective, art and literature are not eternal verities but are always open to new definitions. The dominant class in any historical era will have an important influence on definitions of art, and where new trends arise will normally wish to incorporate them into its ideological world.

The theories of Bakhtin, the Jakobson-Tynyanov theses, and the work of Mukařovský pass beyond the 'pure' Russian Formalism of Shklovsky, Tomashevsky and Eikhenbaum, and form a perfect prelude to our chapter on Marxist criticism, which in any case influenced their more sociological interests. The Formalists' isolation of the literary system is evidently at odds with the Marxist subordination of literature to society, but we shall discover that not all Marxist critics follow the harsh anti-formalist line of the Soviet tradition.

Selected Reading

Basic Texts

Bakhtin, Mikhail, *Problems of Dostoevsky's Poetics*, trans. R.W. Rotsel (Ardis, Ann Arbor, 1973).

Bann, Stephen and Bowlt, John E. (eds), *Russian Formalism* (Scottish Academic Press, Edinburgh, 1973).

Lemon, Lee T. and Reis, Marion J. (eds), *Russian Formalist Criticism: Four Essays* (Nebraska University Press, Lincoln, 1965). Contains classic essays, including Shklovsky's on Sterne.

Matejka, Ladislav and Pomorska, Krystyna, (eds), *Readings in Russian Poetics: Formalist and Structuralist Views* (MIT Press, Cambridge, Mass., and London, 1971).

Medvedev, P.N. and Bakhtin, Mikhail, *The Formal Method in Literary Scholarship*, trans. A.J. Wehrle

(Johns Hopkins University Press, Baltimore and London, 1978).

Mukařovský, Jan, *Aesthetic Function, Norm and Value as Social Facts*, trans. M.E. Suino (Michigan University Press, Ann Arbor, 1979).

Introductions

Bennett, Tony, *Formalism and Marxism* (Methuen, London and New York, 1979).

Erlich, Victor, *Russian Formalism: History Doctrine* (3rd edn, Yale University Press, New Haven and London, 1981). The classic introduction.

Jefferson, Ann, 'Russian Formalism' in *Modern Literary Theory, A Comparative Introduction*, Ann Jefferson and David Robey (eds), (Batsford, London, 1982).

Further Reading

Jameson, Fredric *The Prison-House of Language: A Critical Account of Structuralism and Russian Formalism* (Princeton University Press, Princeton, N.J. and London, 1972).

Pike, Christopher (ed), *The Futurists, the Formalists, and the Marxist Critique* (Ink Links, London, 1979). An anthology.

Selden, R., *Criticism and Objectivity* (Allen & Unwin, London, Boston, Sydney, 1984), chap 4, 'Russian Formalism, Marxism and "Relative Autonomy".'

Thompson, E.M., *Russian Formalism and Anglo-American New Criticism* (Mouton, The Hague, 1971).

Trotsky, L., *Literature and Revolution* (Michigan University Press, Ann Arbor, 1960).

CHAPTER TWO

MARXIST THEORIES

Of the kinds of criticism represented in this guide, Marxist criticism has the longest history. Marx himself made important general statements about culture and society in the 1840s. Even so, it is correct to think of Marxist *criticism* as a twentieth-century phenomenon.

The basic tenets of Marxism are no easier to summarise than the essential doctrines of Christianity, but two well-known statements by Marx provide a sufficient point of departure:

> **The Philosophers have only *interpreted* the world in various ways; the point is to *change* it.**
>
> **It is not the consciousness of men that determines their being, but, on the contrary, their social being that determines their consciousness.**

Both statements were intentionally extreme. By contradicting widely accepted doctrines, Marx was trying to put people's thought into reverse gear. First, philosophy has been merely airy contemplation; it is time that it engaged with the real world. Secondly, Hegel and his followers in German philosophy have persuaded us that the world is governed by thought, that the process of history is the gradual dialectical unfolding of the laws of Reason, and that material existence is the expression of an immaterial spiritual essence. People have been led to believe that their ideas, their cultural life, their legal systems, and their religions were the creations of human and divine reason, which should be regarded as the unquestioned guides to human life. Marx reverses this formulation and argues that all mental (ideological) systems are the products of real social and economic existence. The material interests of the dominant social class determine how people see human existence, individual and collective. Legal systems, for example, are not the pure manifestations of human or divine reason, but ultimately reflect the interests of the dominant class in particular historical periods.

In one account, Marx described this view in terms of an architectural metaphor: the 'superstructure' (ideology, politics) rests upon the 'base' (socio-economic relations). To say 'rests upon' is not quite the same as saying 'is caused by'. Marx was arguing that what we call 'culture' is not an independent reality but is inseparable from the historical conditions in which human beings create their material lives; the relations of dominance and subordination (exploitation) which govern the social and economic order of a particular phase of human history will in some sense 'determine' (not 'cause') the whole cultural life of the society.

In its crudest formulations, the theory is evidently far too mechanical. For example, in *The German Ideology* (1846) Marx and Engels talk about morality, religion and philosophy as 'phantoms formed in the brains of men', which are the 'reflexes and echoes' of 'real life-processes'. On the other hand, in a famous series of letters written in the 1890s Engels insists that, while he and Marx always regarded the economic aspect of society as the *ultimate* determinant of other aspects, they also recognised that art, philosophy, and other forms of consciousness are 'relatively autonomous' and possess an independent ability to alter men's existence. After all, how else do Marxists expect to alter people's awareness except by political discourse? Were we to examine the novels of the eighteenth century or the philosophy of the seventeenth century in Europe, we would recognise, if we were Marxists, that these writings arose at particular phases in the development of early capitalist society. The conflict of social classes establishes the ground upon which ideological conflicts arise. Literature and art belong to the ideological sphere, but possess a relationship to ideology which is even less direct than is found in the case of religious, legal, and philosophical systems.

The special status of literature is recognised by Marx in a celebrated passage in his *Grundrisse*, in which the problem of an apparent discrepancy between economic and artistic development is discussed. Greek tragedy is considered a peak of literary development and yet it coincides with a social system and a form of ideology (Greek myth) which are no longer recognisable to modern society. The problem for Marx was to explain how an art and literature produced in a long-obsolete social organisation can still give us aesthetic pleasure and be regarded as 'a standard and unattainable ideal'. He seems to be accepting reluctantly a certain 'timelessness' and 'universality' in literature and art; reluctantly, because this would be a major concession to one of bourgeois ideology's premises. However, it is now possible to see that Marx was simply falling back on received (Hegelian) ways of thinking about literature and art. Our discussion of Mukařovský in the previous chapter established what can now be regarded as a Marxist view: that canons of great literature are socially generated. The 'greatness' of Greek tragedy is not a universal and unchanging fact of existence, but a *value* which must be reproduced from generation to generation.

Even if we reject a privileged status for literature, there remains the question of how far literature's historical development is independent of historical development in general. In his attack on the Russian Formalists in *Literature and Revolution*, Trotsky conceded that literature had its own principles and rules. 'Artistic creation', he admits, is 'a changing and a transformation of reality in accordance with the peculiar laws of art.' He still insists that the 'reality' remains the crucial factor and not the formal games which writers play. Nevertheless, his remarks point forward to a continuing debate in Marxist criticism about the relative importance of literary form and ideological content in literary works.

Soviet Socialist Realism

Marxist criticism written in the West has often been adventurous and exhilarating, but Socialist Realism, as the official Communist 'artistic method', seems drab and blinkered to Western readers. The doctrines expounded by the Union of Soviet Writers (1932–4) were a codification of Lenin's pre-Revolutionary statements as interpreted during the 1920s. The theory addressed certain major questions about the evolution of literature, its reflection of class relations, and its function in society.

As we have seen, when the Revolution of 1917 encouraged the Formalists to continue developing a revolutionary theory of art, there emerged at the same time an orthodox Communist view, which frowned upon formalism and regarded the nineteenth-century tradition of Russian realism as the only suitable foundation for the aesthetics of the new Communist society. The revolutions in European art, music and literature which occurred around 1910 (Picasso, Stravinsky, Schoenberg, T.S. Eliot) were to be regarded by Soviet critics as the decadent products of late capitalist society. The modernist rejection of traditional realism left Socialist Realism as the leading custodian of bourgeois aesthetics! In Stoppard's *Travesties*, the Dadaist poet Tzara complains that 'the odd thing about revolution is that the further left you go politically, the more bourgeois they like their art'. The combination of nineteenth-century aesthetics and revolutionary politics remained the essential recipe of Soviet theory.

The principle of *partinost'* (commitment to the working-class cause of the Party) is derived almost exclusively from Lenin's essay 'Party Organisation and Party Literature' (1905). In my view, there remains some doubt about Lenin's intentions in arguing that, while all writers were free to write what they liked, they could not expect to be published in Party journals unless they were committed to the Party's political line. While this was a reasonable demand to make in the precarious circumstances of 1905, it took on a much more autocratic significance after the Revolution, when the Party controlled publishing.

The quality of *narodnost'* ('popularity') is central to both the aesthetics and the politics. A work of art of any period achieves this quality by expressing a high level of social awareness, revealing a sense of the true social conditions and feelings of a particular epoch. It will also possess a 'progressive' outlook, glimpsing the developments of the future in the lineaments of the present, and giving a sense of the ideal possibilities of social development from the point of view of the mass of working people. In the 1844 'Paris Manuscripts', Marx argues that the capitalist division of labour destroyed an earlier phase of human history in which artistic and spiritual life were inseparable from the processes of material existence, and craftsmen still worked with a sense of beauty. The separation of mental and manual work dissolved the organic unity of spiritual and material activities, with the result that the masses were forced to produce commodities without the joy of creative engagement in their work. Only folk art survived as the people's art. The appreciation of high art was professionalised, dominated by the market economy, and limited to a privileged section of the ruling class. The truly 'popular' art of socialist societies, argued Soviet critics, will be accessible to the masses and will restore their lost wholeness of being.

The theory of the class nature of art (*klassovost'*) is a complex one. In the writings of Marx, Engels and the Soviet tradition, there is a double emphasis—on the writer's commitment or class interests on the one hand, and the social realism of the writer's work on the other. Only the crudest forms of Socialist Realism treat the class nature of art as a simple matter of the writer's explicit class allegiance. In his letter (1888) to Margaret Harkness on her novel *City Girl*, Engels praises her for not writing an explicitly socialist novel. He argues that Balzac, a reactionary supporter of the Bourbon dynasty, provides a more penetrating account of French society in all its economic details than 'all the professed historians, economists and statisticians of the period together'. Balzac's insights into the downfall of the nobility and the rise of the bourgeoisie compelled him to 'go against his own class sympathies and political prejudices'. Realism transcends class sympathies. This argument was to have a powerful influence not only on the theory of Socialist Realism but on later Marxist criticism.

Socialist Realism is considered to be a continuation and development of bourgeois realism at a higher level. Bourgeois writers are judged not according to their class origins or explicit political commitment, but by the extent to which their writings reveal insights into the social developments of their time. The Soviet hostility to modernist novels can best be understood in this context. Karl Radek's contribution to the Soviet Writers' Congress in 1934 posed the choice 'James Joyce or Socialist Realism?'. During a discussion Radek directed a vitriolic attack against another Communist delegate, Herzfelde, who had defended Joyce as a great writer. Radek regards Joyce's experimental technique and his 'petty bourgeois' content as all of a piece. Joyce's preoccupation with the sordid inner life of a trivial individual indicates his profound unawareness of the larger historical forces at work in modern times. For Joyce 'the whole world lies between a cupboard of medieval books, a brothel and a pot house'. He concludes 'if I were to write novels, I would learn how to write them from Tolstoy and Balzac, not from Joyce.'

This admiration for nineteenth-century realism was understandable. Balzac, Dickens, George Eliot, Stendhal and others developed to its furthest extent a literary form which explores the individual's involvement in the entire network of social relations. Modernist writers abandoned this project and began to reflect a more fragmented image of the world, which was often pessimistic and introverted. Nothing could be further from the 'revolutionary romanticism' of the Soviet school, which wanted to project a heroic image. Andrey Zhdanov, who gave the keynote speech at the 1934 Congress, reminded writers that Stalin had called upon then to be the 'engineers of the human soul'. At this stage, the political demands upon writers became crudely insistent. Engels was clearly doubtful of the value of overly committed writing, but Zhdanov dismissed all such doubts: 'Yes, Soviet literature is tendentious, for in epochs of class struggle there is not and cannot be a literature which is not class literature, not tendentious, allegedly non-political'.

Georg Lukács

It is appropriate to consider next the first major Marxist critic, Georg Lukács, since his work is inseparable from orthodox Socialist Realism. It can be argued that he anticipated some of the Soviet doctrines, but, at any rate, he developed the realist approach with great subtlety. He leaned towards the Hegelian side of Marxist thought by treating literary works as reflections of an unfolding system. A realist work must reveal the underlying pattern of contradictions in a social order. His view is Marxist in its insistence on the material and historical nature of the structure of society.

Lukács' use of the term 'reflection' is characteristic of his work as a whole. Rejecting the down-to-earth 'naturalism' of the then recent European novel, he returns to the old realist view that the novel reflects reality, not by rendering its mere surface appearance, but by giving us 'a truer, more complete, more vivid and more dynamic reflection of reality'. To 'reflect' is 'to frame a mental structure' transposed into words. People ordinarily possess a reflection of reality, a consciousness not merely of objects but of human nature and social relationships. Lukács would say that a reflection may be more or less concrete. A novel may conduct a reader 'towards a more concrete insight into reality', which transcends a merely common-sense apprehension of things. A literary work reflects not individual phenomena in isolation, but 'the full process of life'. However, the reader is always aware that the work is not itself reality but rather 'a special form of reflecting reality'.

A 'correct' reflection of reality, therefore, according to Lukács, involves more than the mere rendering of external appearances. Interestingly, his view of reflection undermines at the same time both naturalism and modernism. It seems true to say that a randomly presented sequence of images may be interpreted either as an *objective* and impartial reflection of reality (as Zola and the other exponents of 'naturalism' demonstrated) or as a purely *subjective* impression of reality (as Joyce and Virginia Woolf seem to show). The randomness can be seen either as a property of reality or of perception. Either way, Lukács rejects such merely 'photographic' representation. Instead, he describes the truly realistic work which gives us a sense of the 'artistic necessity' of the images presented; they possess an 'intensive totality' which corresponds to the 'extensive totality' of the world itself. Reality is not a mere flux, a mechanical collision of fragments, but possesses an 'order', which the novelist renders in an 'intensive' form. The writer does not impose an abstract order upon the world, but rather presents the reader with an image of the richness and complexity of life from which emerges a sense of the order within the complexity and subtlety of lived experience. This will be achieved if all the contradictions and tensions of social existence are realised in a formal whole.

Lukács is able to insist on the principle of underlying order and structure because the Marxist tradition borrowed from Hegel the 'dialectical' view of history. Development in history is not random or chaotic, nor is it a straightforward linear progression, but rather a dialectical development. In every social organisation, the prevailing mode of production gives rise to inner contradictions which are expressed in class struggle. The capitalist mode of production developed by destroying the feudal (artisanal) mode, and replacing it with a non-individual, 'socialised' mode of production, which made possible a more efficient productivity (commodity production). However, while the mode of production was socialised, the ownership of the means of production was privatised. Workers who had owned their looms or tools, eventually had nothing to sell but their labour. The inherent contradiction is expressed in the conflict of interest between capitalist and worker. And yet, the private accumulation of capital was the foundation of factory working, and thus the contradiction (privatisation/socialisation) is a necessary unity, which is central to the nature of the capitalist mode of production. The 'dialectical' resolution of the contradiction is always already implied in the contradiction itself: if people are to re-establish control over their labour power, the ownership of the means of production must also be socialised. This brief excursus is intended to show how Lukács' whole view of realism is shaped by the nineteenth-century inheritance of Marxism.

In a series of brilliant works, especially *The Historical Novel* (1937) and *Studies in European Realism* (1950), Lukács refines and extends the orthodox theories of Socialist Realism. However, in *The Meaning of Contemporary Realism* (1957) he advances the Communist attack on modernism. He refuses to deny Joyce the status of a true artist, but asks us to reject his view of history, and especially the way in which Joyce's 'static' view of events is reflected in an epic structure which is itself essentially static. This failure to perceive human existence as part of a dynamic historical environment infects the whole of contemporary modernism, as reflected in the works of writers such as Kafka, Beckett and Faulkner. These writers, argues Lukács, are preoccupied with formal experiment—with montage, inner monologues, the technique of 'stream of consciousness', the use of reportage, diaries, etc. All this formalistic virtuosity is the result of a narrow concern for subjective impressions, a concern which itself stems from the advanced individualism of late capitalism. Instead of an objective realism we have an *angst*-ridden vision of the world. The fullness of history and its social processes are narrowed down to the bleak inner history of absurd existences. This 'attenuation of actuality' is contrasted to the dynamic and developmental view of society to be found in the nineteenth-century precursors of Socialist Realism, who achieve what Lukács calls 'Critical Realism'.

By divorcing the individual from the outer world of objective reality, the modernist writer, in Lukács' view, is compelled to see the inner life of characters as 'a sinister, inexplicable flux', which ultimately also takes on a timeless static quality. Lukács seems unable to accept that in rendering the impoverished and alienated existence of modern subjects some modern writers achieve a kind of realism, or at any rate develop new literary forms and techniques which correspond to modern reality. Insisting on the reactionary nature of modernist *ideology*, he refused to recognise the *literary* possibilities of modernist writings. Because he thought the *content* of modernism was reactionary, he treated modernist *form* as equally unacceptable. During his brief stay in Berlin during the early 1930s, he found himself attacking the use of modernist techniques of montage and reportage in the work of fellow radicals, including the brilliant dramatist Bertold Brecht.

Bertold Brecht

Brecht's early plays were radical, anarchistic and anti-bourgeois, but not anti-capitalist. After reading Marx in about 1926, his youthful iconoclasm was converted to conscious political commitment, although he always remained a maverick and never a Party man. Around 1930 he was writing the so-called *Lehrstücke*, didactic plays intended for working-class audiences, but he was forced to leave Germany when the Nazis took power in 1933. He wrote his major plays in exile, mainly in Scandinavian countries. Later, in America, he was brought before the McCarthy Committee for un-American Activities and finally settled in East Germany in 1949. He had trouble too with the Stalinist authorities of the GDR, who regarded him as both an asset and a liability.

His opposition to Socialist Realism certainly offended the East German authorities. His best known theatrical device, the alienation effect, was partly derived from the Russian Formalists' concept of 'defamiliarisation'. Socialist Realism favoured realistic illusion, formal unity, and 'positive' heroes. He called *his* theory of realism 'anti-Aristotelian', a covert way of attacking the theory of his opponents. Aristotle emphasised the universality and unity of the tragic action, and the identification of audience and hero in empathy which produces a 'catharsis' of emotions. Brecht rejected the entire tradition of 'Aristotelian' theatre. The dramatist should avoid a smoothly interconnected plot and any sense of inevitability or universality. The facts of social injustice needed to be presented as if they were shockingly unnatural and totally surprising. It is all too easy to regard 'the price of bread, the lack of work, the declaration of war as if they were phenomena of nature: earthquakes or floods'.

To avoid lulling the audience into a state of passive acceptance, the illusion of reality must be shattered by the use of the alienation effect. The actors must not lose themselves in their roles or seek to promote a purely empathic audience identification. They must present a role to the audience, as both recognisable and unfamiliar, so that a process of critical assessment can be set in motion. The situation, emotions and dilemmas of the characters must be understood from the outside and presented as strange and problematic. This is not to say that actors should avoid the use of emotion, but only the resort to empathy. This is achieved by 'baring the device', to use a Formalist term. The use of gesture is an important way of externalising a character's emotions. Gesture or action is studied and rehearsed as a device for conveying in a striking way the specific social meaning of a role. One might contrast this with the Stanislavskian 'method acting', which encourages total identification of actor and role. Improvisation rather than calculation is encouraged in order to create a sense of 'spontaneity' and individuality. This foregrounding of a character's inner life allows its social meaning to evaporate. The gestures of a Marlon Brando or a James Dean are personal and idiosyncratic, while a Brechtian actor (for example Peter Lorre or Charles Laughton) performs rather like a clown or mimic, using diagrammatic gestures which *indicate* rather than reveal. In any case, Brecht's plays, in which the 'heroes' are so often ordinary, tough and unscrupulous, do not encourage the cult of personality. Mother Courage, Asdak and Sweik are boldly outlined on an 'epic' canvas: they are remarkably dynamic social beings, but have no focused 'inner' life.

Brecht rejected the kind of formal unity admired by Lukács. Firstly, Brecht's 'epic' theatre, unlike Aristotle's tragic theatre, is composed of loosely linked episodes of the kind to be found in Shakespeare's history plays and eighteenth-century picaresque novels. There are no artificial constraints of time and place, and no 'well-made' plots. Contemporary inspiration came from the cinema (Charlie Chaplin, Buster Keaton, Eisenstein) and modernist fiction (Joyce and Dos Passos). Secondly, Brecht believed that no model of good form could remain in force indefinitely; there are no 'eternal aesthetic laws'. To capture the living force of reality the writer must be willing to make use of every conceivable formal device, old and new. His attitude to Socialist Realism is clear cut: 'We shall take care not to ascribe realism to a particular historical form of novel belonging to a particular period, Balzac's or Tolstoy's, for instance, so as to set up purely formal and literary criteria of realism.' He considered Lukács' desire to enshrine a particular literary form as the only true model for realism to be a dangerous kind of formalism. Brecht would have been the first to admit that, if his own 'alienation effect' were to become a formula for realism, it would cease to be effective. If we copy other realists' methods, we cease to be realists ourselves: 'Methods wear out, stimuli fail. New problems loom up and demand new techniques. Reality alters; to represent it the means of representation must alter too.' These remarks express clearly Brecht's undogmatic and experimental view of theory. However, there is nothing in the least 'liberal' in his rejection of orthodoxy; his restless search for new ways of shaking audiences out of their complacent passivity into active engagement was motivated by a profoundly political commitment to unmasking every new disguise used by the ever-devious capitalist system.

The Frankfurt School and Benjamin

While Brecht and Lukács held conflicting views of realism, the Frankfurt School of Marxist aesthetics rejected realism altogether. The Institute for Social Research at Frankfurt practised what it called 'Critical Theory', which was a wide-ranging form of social analysis which included Marxian and Freudian elements. The leading figures in philosophy and aesthetics were Max Horkheimer, Theodor Adorno and Herbert Marcuse. Exiled in 1933, the Institute was relocated in New York, but finally returned to Frankfurt in 1950 under Adorno and Horkheimer. They regarded the social system, in Hegelian fashion, as a totality in which all the aspects reflected the same essence. Their analysis of modern culture was influenced by the experience of fascism which had achieved total dominance at every level of social existence in Germany. In America they saw a similar 'one-dimensional' quality in the mass culture and the permeation of every aspect of life by commercialism.

Art and literature have a privileged place in the Frankfurt social theory because they remain the only sphere in which the domination of totalitarian society can be resisted. Adorno criticised Lukács' view of realism, arguing that literature, unlike the mind, does not have a direct contact with reality. In Adorno's view, art is set apart from reality; its detachment gives it its special significance and power. Modernist writings are particularly distanced from the reality to which they allude, and this distance gives their work the power of criticising reality. While popular art forms are forced to collude with the economic system which shapes them, *avant-garde* works have the power to 'negate' the reality to which they relate. Because modernist texts reflect the alienated inner lives of individuals, Lukács attacked them as 'decadent' embodiments of late capitalist society and evidence of the writers' inability to transcend the atomistic and fragmented worlds in which they were compelled to live. Adorno argues that art cannot simply reflect the social system, but acts within that reality as an irritant which produces an indirect sort of knowledge: 'Art is the negative knowledge of the actual world.' This can be achieved, he believed, by writing 'difficult' experimental texts and not directly polemical or critical works. The masses, argues Horkheimer, reject the *avant-garde* because it disturbs their unthinking and automatic acquiescence in their manipulation by the social system: 'By making down-trodden humans shockingly aware of their own despair, the work of art announces a freedom which makes them fume.'

Literary form is not simply a unified and compressed reflection of the form of society, as it was for Lukàcs, but a special means of distancing reality and preventing the easy reabsorption of new insights into familiar and consumable packages. Modernists try to disrupt and fragment the picture of modern life rather than master its dehumanising mechanisms. Lukács could see only symptoms of decay in this kind of art and could not recognise its power to *reveal*. Proust's use of *monologue intèrieur* does not just reflect an alienated individualism, but both grasps a 'truth' about modern society (the alienation of the individual) and enables us to see that the alienation is part of an objective social reality. In a complex essay on Samuel Beckett's *Endgame* Adorno meditates on the ways in which Beckett uses form to evoke the emptiness of modern culture. Despite the catastrophes and degradations of twentieth-century history, we persist in behaving as if nothing has changed. We persist in our foolish belief in the old truths of the unity and substantiality of the individual or the meaningfulness of language. The play presents characters who possess only the hollow shells of individuality and the fragmented clichés of a language. The absurd discontinuities of discourse, the pared-down characterisation, and plotlessness, all contribute to the aesthetic effect of distancing the reality to which the play alludes, and thereby giving us a 'negative' knowledge of modern existence.

Marx believed that he had extracted the 'rational kernel' from the 'mystical shell' of Hegel's dialectic. What survives is the dialectical method of understanding the real processes of human history. The Frankfurt School's work has much of the authentic Hegelian subtlety in dialectical thought. The meaning of dialectic in the tradition of Hegel can be summed up as 'the development which arises from the resolution of contradictions inherent in a particular aspect of reality'. Adorno's *Philosophy of Modern Music*, for example, develops a dialectical account of the composer Schoenberg. The composer's 'atonal' revolution arose in a historical context in which the extreme commercialisation of culture destroys the listener's ability to appreciate the formal unity of a classical work. The commercial exploitation of artistic techniques in cinema, advertising, popular music and so on, forces the composer to respond by producing a shattered and fragmented music, in which the very grammar of musical language (tonality) is denied. Each individual note is cut off and cannot be resolved into meaning by the surrounding context. Adorno describes the content of this 'atonal' music in the language of psychoanalysis: the painfully isolated notes express bodily impulses from the unconscious. The new form is related to the individual's loss of conscious control in modern society. By allowing the expression of violent unconscious impulses, Schoenberg's music evades the censor, reason. However, as Fredric Jameson's fine summary shows, the seeds of a new development (the twelve-tone scale) are already latent in this radical atonality:

> For whatever the will toward total freedom, the atonal composer still works in a world of stale tonality and must take his precautions with regard to the past. He must, for example, avoid the kind of consonance or tonal chord which would be likely to reawaken older listening habits, and to reorganise the music into noise or wrong notes. Yet this very danger is enough to awaken in atonality the first principle of a new law or order. For the taboo against accidentally tonal chords carries with it the corollary that the composer should avoid any exaggerated repetition of a single note, for fear such an insistence would ultimately tend to function as a new kind of tonal centre for the ear. It is necessary only to pose the problem of avoiding such repetition in a more formal way for the entire twelve-tone system to show itself upon the horizon.

The dialectic is completed when this new system is related to the new totalitarian organisation of late capitalist imperialism, in which the autonomy of the individual is lost in the massive and monolithic market-system. That is to say, the music is at once a rebellion against a one-dimensional society and also a symptom of an inescapable loss of freedom.

We cannot leave the Frankfurt School without discussing Walter Benjamin, whose brief association with Adorno justifies his inclusion here, even though his brand of Marxism was highly personal. His best-known essay 'The Work of Art in the Age of Mechanical Reproduction' took a view of modern culture which contradicted Adorno's. He argues that modern technical innovations (cinema, radio, telephone, gramophone) have profoundly altered the status of the 'work of art'. Once, it was the special preserve of the privileged bourgeois élite, when artistic works had an 'aura' deriving from their uniqueness. This was especially true of the visual arts, but even in the case of literature this 'aura' survived. The new media totally shatter this quasi-religious feeling about the arts, and profoundly affect the artist's attitude to production. To a greater and greater extent the *reproduction* of art objects (by means of photography or radio transmission) means that they are actually designed for reproducibility. Adorno saw in this only the cheapening of art by commercialisation, but Benjamin thought that the new media finally divorced art from 'ritual' and opened it to politics. Neither have been proved absolutely correct, but Adorno's views seem to have been nearer to a true prediction.

While new technology (film, the press, etc.) might have a revolutionary effect, Benjamin was aware that there was no guarantee of this. In order to wrest them from the hands of the bourgeoisie, it was necessary for socialist writers and artists to become *producers* in their own artistic sphere. Benjamin's views on the nature of art in its own right were close to Brecht's and indeed the clearest account of his thoughts was written with Brecht's plays in mind. Benjamin rejects the idea that revolutionary art is achieved by attending to the correct subject-matter. Instead of being concerned with a work of art's position within the social and economic relations of its time, he asks the question — what is 'the function of a work within the literary production relations of its time'? The artist needs to revolutionise the *artistic* forces of production of his time. And this is a matter of *technique*. Nevertheless, the correct technique will arise in response to a complex historical combination of social and technical changes. Paris, the anonymous great city of the Second Empire is the subject of Baudelaire's and Poe's writings. Their technical innovations are a direct response to the asocial and fragmented conditions of urban existence: 'The original social content of the detective story was the obliteration of the individual's traces in the big-city crowd.' Benjamin writes of a poem by Baudelaire: 'The inner form of these verses is revealed in the fact that in them love itself is recognized as being stigmatized by the big city.'

'Structuralist' Marxism

The intellectual life of Europe during the 1960s was dominated by structuralism. Marxist criticism was not unaffected by this intellectual environment. Both traditions believe that individuals cannot be understood apart from their social existence. Marxists believe that individuals are 'bearers' of positions in the social system and not free agents. Structuralists consider that individual actions and utterances have no meaning apart from the signifying systems which generate them. However, structuralists regard these underlying structures as timeless and self-regulating systems, but Marxists see them as historical, changeable and fraught with contradictions.

Lucien Goldmann, the Rumanian critic, rejected the idea that texts are creations of individual genius and argued that they are based upon 'trans-individual mental structures' belonging to particular groups (or classes). These 'world views' are perpetually being constructed and dissolved by social groups as they adjust their mental image of the world in response to the changing reality before them. Such mental images usually remain ill-defined and half-realised in the consciousness of social agents, but great writers are able to crystallise world views in a lucid and coherent form.

Goldmann's celebrated *Le Dieu Caché* (*The Hidden God*) establishes connections between Racine's tragedies, Pascal's philosophy, a French religious movement (Jansenism) and a social group (the *noblesse de la robe*). The Jansenist world view is tragic: it sees the individual as divided between a hopelessly sinful world and a God who is absent. God has abandoned the world but still imposes an absolute authority upon the believer. The individual is driven into an extreme and tragic solitude. The underlying structure of relationships in Racine's tragedies expresses the Jansenist predicament, which in turn can be related to the decline of the *noblesse de la robe*, a class of court officials who were becoming increasingly isolated and powerless as the absolute monarchy withdrew its financial support. The 'manifest' content of the tragedies appears to have no connection with Jansenism, but at a deeper structural level they share the same form: 'the tragic hero, equidistant from God and from the world, is *radically alone*'. Goldmann believed that his discovery of structural 'homologies' (similarities of form) between various parts of the social order made his social theory distinctively Marxist and distinguished it from its bourgeois equivalent which insisted on dividing the totality of social practices into self-contained and manageable areas of development. In this respect his work was a continuation of the Hegelian Marxism of Lukács.

His later work, especially *Pour une sociologie du roman* (1964) appears to resemble that of the Frankfurt School by focusing on the 'homology' between the structure of the modern novel and the structure of the market economy. He argues that by about 1910 the transition from the 'heroic' age of liberal capitalism to its imperialist phase was well under way. As a consequence the importance of the individual within economic life was drastically reduced. Finally, in the post-1945 period the regulation and management of economic systems by the state and by corporations brought to its fullest development that tendency which Marxists call 'reification' (this refers to the reduction of value to commodity value and the domination of the human world by a world of objects). In the classic novel, objects only had significance in relation to individuals, but, in the novels of Sartre, Kafka and Robbe-Grillet, the world of objects begins to displace the individual. This final stage of Goldmann's writing depended upon a rather crude model of 'superstructure' and 'base', according to which literary structures simply correspond to economic structures. It avoids the depressing pessimism of the Frankfurt School, but lacks their rich dialectical insights.

Louis Althusser, the French Marxist philosopher, has had a major influence on Marxist literary theory especially in France and Britain. His work is clearly related to structuralism and post-structuralism. He rejects the Hegelian revival within Marxist philosophy, and argues that Marx's real contribution to knowledge stems from his 'break' with Hegel. He criticises Hegel's account of 'totality', according to which the essence of the whole is expressed in all its parts. Althusser avoids terms such as 'social system' and 'order', because they suggest a structure with a centre which determines the form of all its emanations. Instead he talks of the 'social formation', which he regards as a 'decentred' structure. Unlike a living organism this structure has no governing principle, no originating seed, no overall unity. The implications of this view are arresting. The various elements (or 'levels') within the social formation are not treated as reflections of one essential level (the economic level for Marxists): the levels possess a 'relative autonomy', and are ultimately determined by the economic level only 'in the last instance' (this complex formulation derives from Engels). The social formation is a structure in which the various levels exist in complex relations of inner contradiction and mutual conflict. This structure of contradictions may be dominated at any given stage by one or other of the levels, but which level it is to be is itself determined ultimately by the economic level. For example, in feudal social formations religion is structurally dominant, but this does not mean that religion is the essence or centre of the structure. Its leading role is itself determined by the economic level, though not directly.

Althusser's views on literature and art also depart significantly from the traditional Marxist position. He refuses to treat art as simply a form of ideology. In 'A Letter on Art', he locates it somewhere between ideology and scientific knowledge. A great work of literature does not give us a properly conceptual understanding of reality but neither does it merely express the ideology of a particular class. He draws upon Engels' arguments about Balzac (see p. 27) and declares that art 'makes us *see*', in a distanced way, 'the ideology from which it is born, in which it bathes, from which it detaches itself as art, and to which it alludes'. Althusser defines ideology as 'a representation of the imaginary relationship of individuals to their real conditions of existence'. The imaginary consciousness helps us to make sense of the world but also masks or represses our real relationship to it. For example, the ideology of 'freedom' promotes the belief in the freedom of all men, including labourers, but it masks the real relationship of liberal capitalist economy. A dominant system of ideology is accepted as a common-sense view of things by the dominated classes and thus the interests of the dominant class are secured. Art, however, achieves 'a retreat' (a fictional distance) from the very ideology which feeds it. In this way a major literary work can transcend the ideology of the writer.

Pierre Macherey's *A Theory of Literary Production* (1966) influenced Althusser's discussion of art and ideology. He begins by adopting an explicitly Marxist model of writing. Rather than treat the text as a 'creation' or a self-contained artifact, he regards it as a 'production' in which a number of disparate materials are worked over and changed in the process. The materials are not 'free implements' to be used consciously to create a controlled and unified work of art. The text, in working the pre-given materials, is never 'aware of what it is doing'. It has, so to speak, an 'unconscious'. When that state of consciousness we call an ideology enters the text it takes on a different form. Ideology is normally lived as if it were totally natural, as if its imaginary and fluid discourse gives a perfect and unified explanation of reality. Once it is worked into a text, all its contradictions and gaps are exposed. The realist writer intends to unify all the elements in the text, but the work that goes on in the textual process inevitably produces certain lapses and omissions which correspond to the incoherence of the ideological discourse it uses: 'for in order to say anything, there are other things *which must not be said*'. The literary critic is not concerned to show how all the parts of the work fit together, or to harmonise and smooth over any apparent contradictions. Like a psychoanalyst, the critic attends to the text's unconscious—to what is unspoken and inevitably suppressed.

How would this approach work? Consider Defoe's novel, *Moll Flanders*. In the early eighteenth century, bourgeois ideology smoothed over the contradictions between moral and economic requirements; that is, between, on the one hand, a providential view of human life which requires the deferment of immediate gratification for a long-term gain, and on the other an economic individualism which drains all value from human relations and fixes it solely in commodities. Set to work in *Moll Flanders* this ideological discourse is represented so that its contradictions are exposed. The operation of literary form on ideology produces this effect of incoherence. The literary use of Moll as narrator itself involves a double perspective. She tells her story prospectively and retrospectively: she is both a participant who relishes her selfish life as prostitute and thief, and a moraliser who relates her sinful life as a warning to others. The two perspectives are symbolically merged in the episode of Moll's successful business speculation in Virginia where she founds her enterprise upon the ill-gotten gains which were kept secured during her Newgate imprisonment. This economic success is *also* her reward for repenting of her evil life. In this way literary form 'congeals' the fluid discourse of ideology: by giving it formal substance the text shows up the flaws and contradictions in the ideology it uses. The writer does not *intend* this effect since it is produced so to speak 'unconsciously' by the text.

Macherey has recently adopted a more sociological attitude to cultural criticism and places greater emphasis on the educational system as the main source of literary value. He no longer accepts the privileged status accorded to art and literature by Goldmann and Althusser.

Recent developments: Eagleton and Jameson

Marxist theory in the United States has been dominated by the Hegelian inheritance of the Frankfurt School. Given the unfriendly ideological climate of the States, only the rarefied philosophical writings of Adorno and Horkheimer were able to take firm root (the journal *Telos* is the standard-bearer of this tradition). The revival of Marxist criticism in Britain (in decline since the 1930s) was fuelled by the 1968 'troubles' and by the ensuing influx of continental ideas (*New Left Review* was an important channel). A major theorist emerged in response to the specific conditions at work in each country. Fredric Jameson's *Marxism and Form* (1971) and *The Prison-House of Language* (1972) displayed dialectical skills worthy of a Marxist-Hegelian philosopher. Terry Eagleton's *Criticism and Ideology* (1976) built upon the anti-Hegelian Marxism of Althusser and Macherey, and produced an impressive critique of the British critical tradition and a radical revaluation of the development of the English novel. More recently, Jameson (in *The Political Unconscious*, 1981) and Eagleton (in *Walter Benjamin or Towards a Revolutionary Criticism*, 1981) both respond inventively to the challenge of post-structuralism, and show a remarkable resourcefulness and a willingness to modify their earlier positions.

In *Criticism and Ideology* Eagleton begins by exorcising from the body of criticism the spirit of F.R. Leavis and Raymond Williams. Williams, undoubtedly the most versatile British Marxist critic, acknowledged his affiliation to Marxism only late in his career. His early work, notably *Culture and Society 1780–1950* (1958) and *The Long Revolution* (1961), examined the humane, socialist potential of past engagements with industrial society, filtering the literature and social criticism of the past through the specific perspective of his own experience as a Welsh railwayman's son. Williams believed then that Marx's base-superstructure formula was abstract and could not embrace the interwoven texture of 'lived experience'. Eagleton invokes Althusser's arguments against 'empiricism' (the appeal to immediate experience) to demonstrate Williams's inability to make a true 'break' into theory. His key concepts, a 'whole way of life' and a 'structure of feeling', both suggest an unwillingness to distinguish theoretically between subjective experience and the objective social conditions of such experience.

Eagleton, like Althusser, argues that criticism must break with its 'ideological prehistory' and become a 'science'. The central problem is to define the relationship between literature and ideology, because in his view texts do not reflect historical reality but rather work upon ideology to produce an *effect* of the 'real'. The text may appear to be free in its relation to reality (it can invent characters and situations at will), but it is not free in its use of ideology. 'Ideology' here refers not to conscious political doctrines but to all those systems of representation (aesthetic, religious, judicial and others) which shape the individual's mental picture of lived experience. The meanings and perceptions produced in the text are a reworking of ideology's own working of reality. This means that the text works on reality at two removes. Eagleton goes on to deepen the theory by examining the complex layering of ideology from its most general pre-textual forms to the ideology of the text itself. He rejects Althusser's view that literature can distance itself from ideology; it is a complex reworking of already existing ideological discourses. However, the literary result is not merely a reflection of other ideological discourses but a special *production* of ideology. For this reason criticism is not concerned with just the laws of literary form or the theory of ideology but rather with 'the laws of the production of ideological discourses as literature'.

Eagleton surveys a sequence of novels from George Eliot to D.H. Lawrence in order to demonstrate the interrelations between ideology and literary form. He argues that nineteenth-century bourgeois ideology blended a sterile utilitarianism with a series of organicist concepts of society (mainly deriving from the Romantic humanist tradition). As Victorian capitalism became more 'corporatist' it needed bolstering up by the sympathetic social and aesthetic organicism of the Romantic tradition. Eagleton examines each writer's ideological situation and analyses the contradictions which develop in their thinking and the attempted resolutions of the contradictions in their writings. For example, he argues that Lawrence was influenced by Romantic humanism in his belief that the novel reflects the fluidity of life undogmatically, and that society too is ideally an organic order as against the alien capitalist society of modern England. After the destruction of liberal humanism in the First World War Lawrence developed a dualistic pattern of 'female' and 'male' principles. This antithesis is developed and reshuffled in the various stages of his work, and finally resolved in the characterisation of Mellors (*Lady Chatterley's Lover*) who combines impersonal 'male' power and 'female' tenderness. This contradictory combination, which takes various forms in the novels, can be related to a 'deep-seated ideological crisis' within contemporary society.

The impact of post-structuralist thought produced a radical change in Eagleton's work in the late 1970s. His attention shifted from the 'scientific' attitude of Althusser towards the revolutionary thought of Brecht and Benjamin. This shift had the effect of throwing Eagleton back towards the classic Marxist revolutionary theory of the *Theses on Feuerbach* (1845): 'The question whether objective truth can be attributed to human thinking is not a question of theory but is a *practical* question. . . The philosophers have only *interpreted* the world in various ways; the point is to *change* it.' Eagleton believes that 'deconstructive' theories, as developed by Derrida, Paul de Man and others (see chapter 4), can be used to undermine all certainties, all fixed and absolute forms of knowledge. On the other hand, he criticises deconstruction for its petit-bourgeois denial of 'objectivity' and material 'interests' (especially class interests). This contradictory view can be understood if we note that Eagleton now espouses Lenin's and not Althusser's view of theory: correct theory 'assumes final shape only in close connection with the practical activity of a truly mass and truly revolutionary movement'. The tasks of Marxist criticism are now set up by politics and not by philosophy: the critic must dismantle received notions of 'literature' and reveal their ideological role in shaping the subjectivity of readers. As a socialist the critic must 'expose the rhetorical structures by which non-socialist works produce politically undesirable effects' and also 'interpret such works where possible "against the grain"', so that they work for socialism.

Eagleton's major book of this phase is *Walter Benjamin or Towards a Revolutionary Criticism* (1981). The odd materialist mysticism of Benjamin is read 'against the grain' to produce a revolutionary criticism. His view of history involves a violent grasping of historical meaning from a past which is always threatened and obscured by reactionary and repressive memory. When the right (political) moment comes, a voice from the past can be seized and appropriated to its 'true' purpose. Brecht's plays, admired by Benjamin, often reread history 'against the grain', breaking down the relentless narratives of history and opening the past to re-inscription. For example, Shakespeare's *Coriolanus* and Gay's *Beggar's Opera* are 'rewritten' in order to expose their potential socialist meanings. (Brecht characteristically insisted that we must go beyond mere empathy with Shakespeare's self-regarding 'hero' and must be able to appreciate the tragedy not only of Coriolanus but also 'specifically of the plebs'.)

Eagleton applauds Brecht's radical and opportunistic approach to meaning: 'a work may be realist in June and anti-realist in December'. Eagleton frequently alludes to Perry Anderson's *Considerations on Western Marxism* (1976) which shows how the development of Marxist theory always reflects the state of the working-class struggle. Eagleton believes, for example, that the Frankfurt School's highly 'negative' critique of modern culture was a response first to fascist domination in Europe, and then to the pervasive capitalist domination in the United States, but that it was also the result of the School's theoretical and practical divorce from the working-class movement. However, what makes Eagleton's revolutionary criticism distinctively *modern* is his tactical deployment of the Freudian theories of Lacan and the powerful deconstructive philosophy of Jacques Derrida (see chapter 4).

In America, where the labour movement has been partially corrupted and totally excluded from political power, the appearance of a major Marxist theorist is an important event. On the other hand, if we keep in mind Eagleton's point about the Frankfurt School and American society, it is not without significance that Fredric Jameson's work has been deeply influenced by that School. In *Marxism and Form* (1971) he explores the dialectical aspect of Marxist theories of literature. After a fine sequence of studies (Adorno, Benjamin, Marcuse, Bloch, Lukács, and Sartre) he presents the outline of a 'dialectical criticism'.

Jameson believes that in the post-industrial world of monopoly capitalism the only kind of Marxism which has any purchase on the situation is a Marxism which explores the 'great themes of Hegel's philosophy—the relationship of part to whole, the opposition between concrete and abstract, the concept of totality, the dialectic of appearance and essence, the interaction between subject and object'. For dialectical thought there are no fixed and unchanging 'objects'; an 'object' is inextricably bound up with a larger whole, and is also related to a thinking mind which is itself part of a historical situation. Dialectical criticism does not isolate individual literary works for analysis; an individual is always part of a larger structure (a tradition or a movement) or part of a historical situation. The dialectical critic has no pre-set categories to apply to literature and will always be aware that his or her chosen categories (style, character, image, etc.) must be understood ultimately as an aspect of the critic's own historical situation. Jameson shows that Wayne Booth's *Rhetoric of Fiction* (1961) is lacking in a proper dialectical self-awareness. Booth adopts the concept of 'point of view' in the novel, a concept which is profoundly modern in its implied relativism and rejection of any fixed or absolute viewpoint or standard of judgement. However, by defending the specific point of view represented by the 'implied author', Booth tries to restore the certainties of the nineteenth-century novel, a move which reflects a nostalgia for a time of greater middle-class stability in an orderly class system. A Marxist dialectical criticism will always recognise the historical origins of its own concepts and will never allow the concepts to ossify and become insensitive to the pressure of reality. We can never get outside our subjective existence in time, but we *can* try to break through the hardening shell of our ideas 'into a more vivid apprehension of reality itself'.

A dialectical criticism will seek to unmask the inner form of a genre or body of texts and will work from the surface of a work inward to the level where literary form is deeply related to the concrete. Taking Hemingway as his example, Jameson contends that the 'dominant category of experience' in the novels is the process of writing itself. Hemingway discovered that he could produce a certain kind of bare sentence which could do two things well: register movement in nature (things) and suggest the tension of resentments between people. The achieved writing skill is linked conceptually with other human skills which are expressed in relation to the natural world (especially blood sports). The Hemingway cult of *machismo* reflects the American ideal of technical skill but rejects the alienating conditions of industrial society by transposing human skill into the sphere of leisure. Hemingway's laid-bare sentences cannot gain access to the complex fabric of American society and so his novels are directed to the thinned-down reality of foreign cultures in which individuals stand out with the 'cleanness of objects' and can therefore be contained in Hemingway's sentences. In this way Jameson shows how literary form is deeply engaged with a concrete reality.

His *The Political Unconscious* (1981) retains the earlier dialectical conception of theory but also assimilates various conflicting traditions of thought (structuralism, post-structuralism, Freud, Althusser, Adorno) in an impressive and still recognisably Marxist synthesis. Jameson argues that the fragmented and alienated condition of human society implies an original state of Primitive Communism in which both life and perception were 'collective'. When humanity suffered a sort of Blakean Fall, the very human senses themselves established separate spheres of specialisation. A painter treats sight as a specialised sense; his or her paintings are a symptom of alienation. However, they are also a compensation for the loss of a world of original fullness: they provide colour in a colourless world.

All ideologies are 'strategies of containment' which allow society to provide an explanation of itself which suppresses the underlying contradictions of History; it is History itself (the brute reality of economic Necessity) which imposes this strategy of repression. Literary texts work in the same way: the solutions which they offer are merely symptoms of the suppression of History. Jameson cleverly uses A.J. Greimas' structuralist theory (the 'semiotic rectangle') as an analytic tool for his own purposes. Textual strategies of containment present themselves as formal patterns. Greimas' structuralist system provides a complete inventory of possible human relations (sexual, legal, etc.) which, when applied to a text's strategies, will allow the analyst to discover the possibilities which are *not said*. This 'not said' is the repressed History.

Jameson also develops a powerful argument about narrative and interpretation. He believes that narrative is not just a literary form or mode but an essential 'epistemological category'; reality presents itself to the human mind only in the form of stories. Even a scientific theory is a form of story. Further, all narratives require interpretation. Here Jameson is answering the common post-structuralist argument against 'strong' interpretation. Deleuze and Guattari (in *The Anti-Oedipus*) attack all 'transcendent' interpretation, allowing only 'immanent' interpretation which avoids imposing a strong 'meaning' on a text. Transcendent interpretation tries to master the text and in so doing *impoverishes* its true complexity. Jameson cunningly takes the example of New Criticism (a self-declared immanentist approach), and shows that it is in fact transcendent, its master code being 'humanism'. He concludes that all interpretations are necessarily transcendent and ideological. In the end, all we can do is to use ideological concepts as a means of transcending ideology.

Jameson's 'political unconscious' takes from Freud the essential concept of 'repression', but raises it from the individual to the collective level. The function of ideology is to repress 'revolution'. Not only do the oppressors need this political unconscious but also the oppressed who would find their existence unbearable if 'revolution' were not repressed. To analyse a novel we need to establish an absent cause (the 'not-revolution'). Jameson proposes a critical method which includes three 'horizons' (a level of immanent analysis, using Greimas for example, a level of social-discourse analysis, and an epochal level of Historical reading). The third horizon of reading is based upon Jameson's complex rethinking of Marxist models of society. Broadly, he accepts Althusser's view of the social totality as a 'decentred structure' in which various levels develop in 'relative autonomy' and work on different time-scales (the coexistence of feudal and capitalist time-scales, for example). This complex structure of antagonistic and out-of-key modes of production is the heterogeneous History which is mirrored in the heterogeneity of texts. Jameson is here answering the post-structuralists who would abolish the distinction between text and reality by treating reality itself as just more text. He shows that the textual heterogeneity can be understood only as it relates to social and cultural heterogeneity *outside* the text. In this he preserves a space for a Marxist analysis.

In the course of this chapter we have referred to 'structuralist' Marxism. The economic writings of Karl Marx themselves have been regarded as essentially structuralist. Before turning to structuralism itself, it is worth emphasising that the differences between Marxist and structuralist theories are much greater than the similarities. For Marxism the ultimate ground of its theories is the material and historical existence of human societies; but for structuralists the final bedrock is the nature of language. While Marxist theories are about the historical changes and conflicts which arise in society and appear indirectly in literary form, structuralism studies the internal working of systems divorced from their historical existence.

Selected Reading

Basic Texts

Adorno, Theodor W., *Prisms* (Neville Spearman, London, 1967).

Adorno, Theodor W., and Horkheimer, Max, *Dialectic of Enlightenment* (Allen Lane, London, 1972).

Baxandall, Lee, and Morawski, Stefan, *Marx and Engels on Literature and Art* (International General, N.Y., 1973).

Benjamin, Walter, *Illuminations* (Schocken, New York; Cape, London, 1970).

Benjamin, Walter, *Charles Baudelaire: A Lyric Poet in the Era of High Capitalism*, trans. H. Zohn (New Left Books, London, 1973).

Benjamin, Walter, *Understanding Brecht*, trans. A. Bostock (New Left Books, 1973).

Craig, David (ed.), *Marxists on Literature* (Harmonds-

worth, Penguin, 1975).
Eagleton, Terry, *Criticism and Ideology* (New Left Books, London, 1976).
Eagleton, Terry, *Walter Benjamin or Towards a Revolutionary Criticism* (New Left Books, London, 1981).
Goldmann, Lucien, *The Hidden God* (Routledge & Kegan Paul, London, 1964).
Jameson, Fredric, *Marxism and Form* (Princeton University Press, Princeton, 1971).
Jameson, Fredric (ed.), *Aesthetics and Politics* (New Left Books, London, 1977).
Jameson, Fredric, *The Political Unconscious: Narrative as a Socially Symbolic Act* (Cornell University Press, Ithaca, 1981).
Lukács, Georg, *The Historical Novel* (Merlin Press, London, 1962).
Lukács, Georg, *The Meaning of Contemporary Realism* (Merlin Press, London, 1963).
Lukács, Georg, *Writer and Critic and Other Essays* (Merlin Press, London, 1970).
Lukács, Georg, *Studies in European Realism* (Merlin Press, London, 1972).
Macherey, Pierre, *A Theory of Literary Production*, trans. G. Wall (Routledge & Kegan Paul, London, Henley and Boston, 1978).
Marcuse, Herbert, *One-Dimensional Man* (Beacon, Boston; Sphere, London, 1964).
Sartre, Jean-Paul, *What is Literature?* (Philosophical Library, New York, 1949).
Willett, John (ed.), *Brecht on Theatre* (Methuen, London, 1964).
Williams, Raymond, *Problems in Materialism and Culture* (New Left Books, London, 1980).

Introductions

Arvon, Henri, *Marxist Aesthetics*, trans. H. Lane (Cornell University Press, Ithaca and London, 1973).
Belsey, Catherine, *Critical Practice* (Methuen, London, 1980).
Dowling, William, C., *Jameson, Althusser, Marx: an Intro-*

duction to the Political Unconscious* (Methuen, London, and Cornell University Press, Ithaca, 1984).

Eagleton, Terry, *Marxism and Literary Criticism* (Methuen, London, 1976).

Forgacs, David, 'Marxist Literary Theories', in A. Jefferson and D. Robey (eds), *Modern Literary Theory* (Batsford, London, 1982).

Laing, Dave, *The Marxist Theory of Art : An Introductory Survey* (Harvester Press, Hassocks, Sussex, 1978).

Lifshitz, Mikhail, *The Philosophy of Art of Karl Marx,* trans. R.B. Winn (Pluto Press, London, 1973; Russian edn, 1933).

Further Reading

James, C. Vaughan, *Soviet Socialist Realism : Origins and Theory* (Macmillan, London and Basingstoke, 1973).

Jay, Martin, *The Dialectical Imagination: A History of the Frankfurt School* (Heinemann, London, 1973).

Slaughter, Cliff, *Marxism, Ideology and Literature* (Macmillan, London and Basingstoke, 1980).

Williams, Raymond, *Marxism and Literature* (Oxford University Press, Oxford, 1977).

Wolff, Janet, *The Social Production of Art* (Macmillan, London and Basingstoke, 1981).

CHAPTER THREE

STRUCTURALIST THEORIES

New ideas often provoke philistine and anti-intellectual reactions, and this has been especially true of the reception accorded the theories which go under the name of 'structuralism'. Structuralist approaches to literature challenge some of the most cherished beliefs of the ordinary reader. The literary work, we have long felt, is the child of an author's creative life, and expresses the author's essential self. The text is the place where we enter into a spiritual or humanistic communion with an author's thoughts and feelings. Another fundamental assumption which readers often make is that a good book tells the truth about human life—that novels and plays try to tell us how things are. However, structuralists have tried to persuade us that the author is 'dead' and that literary discourse has no truth function. In a review of a book by Jonathan Culler, John Bayley spoke for the anti-structuralists when he declared 'but the sin of semiotics is to attempt to destroy our sense of truth in fiction ... In a good story, truth precedes fiction and remains separable from it.' In a 1968 essay, Roland Barthes put the structuralist view very powerfully, and argued that writers only have the power to mix already existing writings, to reassemble or redeploy them; writers cannot use writing to 'express' themselves, but only to draw upon that immense dictionary of language and culture which is 'always already written' (to use a favourite Barthean phrase). It would not be misleading to use the term 'anti-humanist' to describe the spirit of structuralism. Indeed the word has been used by structuralists themselves to emphasise their opposition to all forms of literary criticism in which the human subject is the source and origin of literary meaning.

The linguistic background

Saussure's two key ideas provide new answers to the questions 'What is the object of linguistic investigation?' and 'What is the relationship between words and things?' He makes a fundamental distinction between *langue* and *parole*—between the language *system*, which pre-exists actual examples of language, and the individual *utterance*. *Langue* is the social aspect of language: it is the shared system which we (unconsciously) draw upon as speakers. *Parole* is the individual realisation of the system in actual instances of language. This distinction is essential to all later structuralist theories. The proper object of linguistic study is the system which underlies any particular human signifying practice, not the individual utterance. This means that, if we examine specific poems or myths or economic practices, we do so in order to discover what system of rules—what grammar—is being used. After all, human beings use speech quite differently from parrots: the former evidently have a grasp of a system of rules which enable them to produce an infinite number of well-formed sentences; parrots do not.

Saussure rejected the idea that language is a word-heap gradually accumulated over time and that its primary function is to refer to things in the world. In his view, words are not symbols which correspond to referents, but rather are 'signs' which are made up of two parts (like two sides of a sheet of paper): a mark, either written or spoken, called a 'signifier', and a concept (what is 'thought' when the mark is made), called a 'signified'. The view he is rejecting may be represented thus:

$$\text{SYMBOL} = \text{THING}$$

Saussure's model is as follows:

$$\text{SIGN} = \frac{\text{signifier}}{\text{signified}}$$

'Things' have no place in the model. The elements of language acquire meaning not as the result of some connection between words and things, but only as parts of a system of relations. Consider the sign-system of traffic lights:

red — amber — green

$$\frac{\text{signifier (`red')}}{\text{signified (stop)}}$$

The sign signifies only within the system 'red=stop / green=go / amber = prepare for red or green'. The relation between signifier and signified is arbitrary: there is no natural bond between red and stop, no matter how natural it may *feel*. Since joining the Common Market the British have had to accept new electrical colour codings which may seen unnatural (now brown, not red, = live; blue, not black, = neutral). Each colour in the traffic system signifies not by asserting a positive univocal meaning but by marking a *difference*, a distinction within a system of opposites and contrasts: traffic-light 'red' is precisely 'not-green'; 'green' is 'not-red'.

Language is one among many sign-systems (some believe it is the fundamental system). The science of such systems is called 'semiotics' or 'semiology'. It is usual to regard structuralism and semiotics as belonging to the same theoretical universe. Structuralism, it must be added, is often concerned with systems which do not involve 'signs' as such (kinship relations, for example) but which can be treated in the same way as sign-systems. The American philosopher C.S. Pierce made a useful distinction between three types of sign: the 'iconic' (where the sign *resembles* its referent; e.g. a picture of a ship or a road-sign for falling rocks); the 'indexical' (where the sign is *associated*, possibly causally, with its referent; e.g. smoke as a sign of fire, or clouds as a sign of rain); and the 'symbolic' (where the sign has an *arbitrary* relation to its referent; e.g. language). The most celebrated modern semiotician is Yuri Lotman of the USSR.

The first major developments in structuralist studies were based upon advances in the study of phonemes, the lowest-level elements in the language system. A phoneme is a meaningful sound, one that is recognised or perceived by a language user. We do not recognise sounds as meaningful bits of noise in their own right, but register them as different in some respects from other sounds. Barthes draws attention to this principle in the title of his most celebrated book *S/Z*, which picks out the two sibilants in Balzac's *Sarrasine (Sarrazine)*, which are differentiated phonemically as *voiced (z)* and *unvoiced (s)*. On the other hand there are differences of raw sound at the phonetic (not phonemic) level which are not 'recognised' in English: the /p/ sound in 'pin' is evidently different from the /p/ sound in 'spin', but English speakers do not recognise a difference: the difference is not recognised in the sense that it does not 'distribute' meaning between words in the language. Even if we said 'sbin', we would probably hear it as 'spin'. The essential point about this view of language is that underlying our use of language is a *system*, a pattern of paired opposites, *binary oppositions.* At the level of the phoneme, these include nasalised/non-nasalised, vocalic/non-vocalic, voiced/unvoiced, tense/lax. In a sense, speakers appear to have internalised a set of rules which manifests itself in their evident *competence* in operating language.

We can observe 'structuralism' of this type at work in the anthropology of Mary Douglas (an example used by Jonathan Culler). She examines the abominations of Leviticus, according to which some creatures are clean and some unclean on an apparently random principle. She solves the problem by constructing the equivalent of a phonemic analysis, according to which two rules appear to be in force: (1) 'cloven-hoofed, cud-chewing ungulates are the model of the proper kind of food for a pastoralist'; animals which only half conform (pig, hare, rock badger) are unclean; (2) another rule applies if the first is not relevant: each creature should be in the element to which it is biologically adapted. So fish without fins are unclean, and so on. At a more complex level, the anthropology of Claude Lévi-Strauss develops a 'phonemic' analysis of myths, rites, kinship structures. Instead of asking questions about the origins or causes of the prohibitions, myths or rites, the structuralist looks for the system of differences which underlies a particular human practice.

As these examples from anthropology show, structuralists try to uncover the 'grammar', 'syntax', or 'phonemic' pattern of particular human systems of meaning, whether they be those of kinship, garments, *haute cuisine*, narrative discourse, myths, or totems. The liveliest examples of such analyses can be found in the earlier writings of Roland Barthes, especially in the wide-ranging *Mythologies* (1957) and *Système de la mode* (1967). The theory of these studies is given in *Elements of Semiology* (1964).

The principle—that human performances presuppose a

received system of differential relations—is applied by Barthes to virtually all social practices; he interprets them as sign-systems which operate on the model of language. Any actual 'speech' (*parole*) presupposes a system (*langue*) which is being used. Barthes recognises that the language system may change, and that changes must be initiated in 'speech'; nevertheless, at any given moment there exists a working system, a set of rules from which all 'speeches' may be derived. To take an example, when Barthes examines the wearing of garments, he sees it not as a matter of personal expression or individual style, but as a 'garment system' which works like a language. He divides the 'language' of garments between 'system' and 'speech' ('syntagm').

System	*Syntagm*
'Set of pieces, parts or details which cannot be worn at the same time on the same part of the body, and whose variation corresponds to a change in the meaning of the clothing: toque—bonnet—hood, etc.'	'Juxtaposition in the same type of dress of different elements: skirt—blouse—jacket.'

To make a garment 'speech', we choose a particular ensemble (syntagm) of pieces each of which could be replaced by other pieces. An ensemble (sports jacket/grey-flannelled trousers/white open-necked shirt) is equivalent to a specific sentence uttered by an individual for a particular purpose; the elements fit together to make a particular kind of utterance and to evoke a meaning or style. No one can actually perform the system itself, but their selection of elements from the sets of garments which make up the system express their *competence* in handling the system. Here is a representation of a culinary example Barthes provides:

System	*Syntagm*
'Set of foodstuffs which have affinities or differences, within which one chooses a dish in view of a certain meaning: the types of entrée, roast or sweet.'	'Real sequence of dishes chosen during meal; menu.'

(a restaurant *à la carte* menu has both levels: entrée and examples)

Structuralist narratology

When we apply the linguistic model to literature, we appear to be sending coals to Newcastle. After all if literature is already linguistic, what is the point of examining it in the light of a linguistic model? Well, for one thing, it would be a mistake to identify 'literature' and 'language'. It is true that literature *uses* language as its medium, but this does not mean that the structure of literature is identical with the structure of language. The units of literary structure do not coincide with those of language. This means that when Todorov advocates a new poetics which will establish a general 'grammar' of literature, he is talking about the underlying rules governing literary practice. On the other hand, structuralists agree that literature has a special relationship with language: it draws attention to the very nature and specific properties of language. In this respect structuralist poetics are closely related to Formalism.

Structuralist narrative theory develops from certain elementary linguistic analogies. Syntax (the rules of sentence construction) is the basic model of narrative rules. Todorov and others talk of 'narrative syntax'. The most elementary syntactic division of the sentence unit is between subject and predicate: 'The knight (subject) slew the dragon with his sword (predicate).' Evidently this sentence could be the core of an episode or even an entire tale. If we substitute a name (Launcelot or Gawain) for 'the knight', or 'axe' for 'sword', we retain the same essential structure. By pursuing this analogy between sentence structure and narrative, Vladimir Propp developed his theory of Russian fairy stories.

Propp's approach can be understood if we compare the

'subject' of a sentence with the typical characters (hero, villain, etc.) and the 'predicate' with the typical actions in such stories. While there is an enormous profusion of details, the whole corpus of tales is constructed upon the same basic set of thirty-one 'functions'. A function is the basic unit of the narrative 'language' and refers to the significant actions which form the narrative. These follow a logical sequence, and although no tale includes them all, in every tale the functions always remain in sequence. The last group of functions is as follows:

25. A difficult task is proposed to the hero.
26. The task is resolved.
27. The hero is recognised.
28. The false hero or villain is exposed.
29. The false hero is given a new appearance.
30. The villain is punished.
31. The hero is married and ascends the throne.

It is not difficult to see that these functions are present not just in Russian fairy tales or even non-Russian tales, but also in comedies, myths, epics, romances, and indeed stories in general. However, Propp's functions have a certain archetypal simplicity which requires elaboration when applied to more complex texts. For example, in the Oedipus myth, Oedipus is set the task of solving the riddle of the sphinx; the task is resolved; the hero is recognised; he is married and ascends the throne. However, Oedipus is also the false hero and the villain; he is exposed (he murdered his father on the way to Thebes and married his mother, the queen), and punishes himself. Propp had added seven 'spheres of action' or roles to the thirty-one functions: villain, donor (provider), helper, princess (sought-after person) and her father, dispatcher, hero (seeker or victim), false hero. The tragic myth of Oedipus requires the substitution of 'mother/queen and husband' for 'princess and her father'. One character can play several roles, or several characters can play the same role. Oedipus is both hero, provider (he averts Thebes' plague by solving the riddle), false hero, and even villain.

Claude Lévi-Strauss, the structuralist anthropologist, analyses the Oedipus myth in a manner which is truly structuralist in its use of the linguistic model. He calls the units of myth 'mythemes' (compare phonemes and morphemes in linguistics). They are organised in binary oppositions (see p. 54) like the basic linguistic units. The general opposition underlying the Oedipus myth is between two views of the origin of human beings: (i) that they are born from the earth (one); (ii) that they are born from coition (two). Several mythemes are grouped on one side or the other of the antithesis between (i) the *over*valuation of kinship ties (Oedipus marries his mother; Antigone buries her brother unlawfully); and (ii) the *under*valuation of kinship (Oedipus kills his father; Eteocles kills his brother). Lévi-Strauss is not interested in the narrative *sequence*, but in the structural *pattern* which gives the myth its meaning. He looks for the 'phonemic' structure of myth. He believes that this linguistic model will uncover the basic structure of the human mind—the structure which governs the way human beings shape all their institutions, artifacts, and their forms of knowledge.

A.J. Greimas, in his *Sémantique Structurale* (1966), offers an elegant streamlining of Propp's theory. While Propp focused on a single genre, Greimas aims to arrive at the universal 'grammar' of narrative by applying to it a semantic analysis of sentence structure. In place of Propp's seven 'spheres of action' he proposes three pairs of binary oppositions which include all six roles (*actants*) he requires:

Subject/Object
Sender/Receiver
Helper/Opponent

The pairs describe three basic patterns which perhaps recur in all narrative:

1. Desire, search, or aim (subject/object)
2. Communication (sender-receiver)
3. Auxiliary support or hindrance (helper/opponent)

If we apply these to Sophocles' *Oedipus the King*, we arrive at a more penetrating analysis than when using Propp's categories:

1. O. searches for the murderer of Laius. Ironically he searches for himself (he is both subject and object).
2. Apollo's oracle predicts O's sins. Teiresias, Jocasta, the messenger and the herdsman all, knowingly or not, confirm its truth. The play is about O's misunderstanding of the message.
3. Teiresias and Jocasta try to prevent O. from discovering the murderer. The messenger and the herdsman unwittingly assist him in the search. O. himself obstructs the correct interpretation of the message.

It can be seen at a glance that Greimas reworking of Propp is in the direction of the 'phonemic' patterning we saw in Lévi-Strauss. In this respect Greimas is more truly 'structuralist' than the Russian Formalist Propp, in that the former thinks in terms of *relations* between entities rather than of the character of entities in themselves. In order to account for the various narrative sequences which are possible he reduces Propp's thirty-one functions to twenty, and groups them into three structures (syntagms): 'contractual', 'performative', and 'disjunctive'. The first, the most interesting, is concerned with the establishing or breaking of contracts or rules. Narratives may employ either of the following structures:

contract (or prohibition) → violation → punishment
lack of contract (disorder) → establishment of contract (order)

The Oedipus narrative has the first structure: he violates the prohibition against patricide and incest, and punishes himself.

The work of Tzvetan Todorov is a summation of Propp, Greimas and others. All the syntactic rules of language are restated in their narrative guise—rules of agency, predication, adjectival and verbal functions, mood and aspect, and so on. The minimal unit of narrative is the 'proposition', which can be either an 'agent' (e.g. a person) or a 'predicate' (e.g. an action). The propositional structure of a narrative can be described in the most abstract and universal fashion. Using Todorov's method, we might have the following propositions:

X is king	X marries Y
Y is X's mother	X kills Z
Z is X's father	

These are some of the propositions which make up the narrative of the Oedipus myth. For X read Oedipus; for Y, Jocasta; for Z, Laius. The first three propositions denominate agents, the first and the last two contain predicates (to be a king, to marry, to kill). Predicates may work like adjectives and refer to static states of affairs (to be a king), or they may operate dynamically like verbs to indicate transgressions of law and are therefore the most dynamic types of proposition. Having established the smallest unit (proposition), Todorov describes two higher levels of organisation: the *sequence* and the *text*. A group of propositions forms a sequence. The basic sequence is made up of five propositions which describe a certain state which is disturbed and then re-established albeit in altered form. The five propositions may be designated thus:

Equilibrium^1 (e.g. Peace)
Force^1 (Enemy invades)
Disequilibrium (War)
Force^2 (Enemy is defeated)
Equilibrium^2 (Peace on new terms)

Finally a succession of sequences forms a text. The sequences may be organised in a variety of ways, by embedding (story within a story, digression, etc.), by linking (a string of sequences), or by alternation (interlacing of sequences), or by a mixture of these. Todorov provides his most vivid examples in a study of Boccaccio's *Decameron (Grammaire du Décaméron*, 1969). His attempt to establish the universal syntax of narrative has all the air of a scientific theory. As we shall see, it is precisely against this confidently objective stance that the post-structuralists react.

Gérard Genette developed his complex and powerful theory of discourse in the context of a study of Proust's *À la recherche du temps perdu*. He refines the Russian Formalist distinction between 'story' and 'plot' (see chapter one) by dividing narrative into three levels: story (*histoire*), discourse (*récit*), and *narration*. For example, in *Aeneid* II Aeneas is the story-teller addressing his audience (*narration*); he presents a *discourse*; and his discourse represents events in which he appears as a character (*story*). These dimensions of narrative are related by three aspects, which Genette derives from the three qualities of the verb: *tense*, *mood*, and *voice*. To take just one example, his distinction between 'mood' and 'voice' neatly clarifies problems which can arise from the familiar notion of 'point-of-view'. We often fail to distinguish between the voice of the narrator and the perspective (mood) of a character. In *Great Expectations* Pip presents the perspective of his younger self through the narrative voice of his older self.

Genette's essay on 'Frontiers of narrative' (1966) provided an overview of the problems of narration which has not been bettered. He considers the problem of narrative theory by exploring three binary oppositions. The first, 'diegesis and mimesis' (narrative and representation) occurs in Aristotle's *Poetics* and presupposes a distinction between simple narrative (what the author says in his own voice as author) and direct imitation (when the author speaks in the person of a character). Genette shows that the distinction cannot be sustained, since if one *could* have direct imitation involving a pure representation of what someone actually said, it would be like a Dutch painting in which actual objects were included on the canvas. He concludes: 'Literary representation, the *mimesis* of the ancients, is not, therefore, narrative plus "speeches": it is narrative and only narrative.' The second opposition, 'narration and description', presupposes a distinction between an active and a contemplative aspect of narration. The first is to do with actions and events, the second with objects or characters. 'Narration' appears, at first, to be essential, since events and actions are the essence of a story's temporal and dramatic content, while 'description' appears to be ancillary and ornamental. 'The man went over to the table and picked up a knife' is dynamic and profoundly narrativistic. However, having established the distinction, Genette immediately dissolves it by pointing out that the nouns and verbs in the sentence are also descriptive. If we change 'man' to 'boy', or 'table' to 'desk', or 'picked up' to 'grabbed', we have altered the description. Finally, the opposition 'narrative and discourse' distinguishes between a pure telling in which 'no one speaks' and a telling in which we are aware of the person who is speaking. Once again, Genette cancels the opposition by showing that there can never be a pure narrative devoid of 'subjective' colouration. However transparent and unmediated a narrative may appear to be, the signs of a judging mind are rarely absent. Narratives are nearly always impure in this sense, whether the element of 'discourse' enters via the voice of the narrator (Fielding, Cervantes), a character–narrator (Sterne), or through epistolary discourse (Richardson). Genette believes that narrative reached its highest degree of purity in Hemingway and Hammett, but that with the *nouveau roman* narrative began to be totally swallowed up in the writer's own discourse. In our next chapter we shall see that Genette's theoretical approach, with its positing and cancellation of oppositions, opens the door to the 'deconstructive' philosophy of Jacques Derrida.

If the reader has followed me so far, he or she may well object that structuralist poetics seems to have little to offer the practising critic. It is perhaps not without significance that fairy stories, myths, and detective stories often feature as examples in structuralist writings. Such studies aim to define the *general principles* of literary structure and not to provide interpretations of individual texts. A fairy story will provide clearer examples of the essential narrative grammar of all stories than will *King Lear* or *Ulysses.*

Metaphor and metonymy

There are some instances when a structuralist theory provides the practical critic with a fertile ground for interpretative applications. This is true of Roman Jakobson's study of 'aphasia' (speech defect) and its implications for poetics. He starts by stating the fundamental distinction between horizontal and vertical dimensions of language, a distinction related to that between *langue* and *parole*. Taking Barthes garments system as an example, we note that in the vertical dimension we have an inventory of elements that may be substituted for one another: toque—bonnet—hood; in the horizontal dimension, we have elements chosen from the inventory to form an actual sequence (skirt—blouse—jacket). Thus a given sentence may be viewed either vertically or horizontally: (1) each element is *selected* from a set of possible elements and could be substituted for another in the set; (2) the elements are *combined* in a sequence, which constitutes a *parole*. This distinction applies at all levels—phoneme, morpheme, word, sentence. Jakobson noticed that aphasic children appeared to lose the ability to operate one or other of these dimensions. One type of aphasia exhibited 'contiguity disorder', the inability to combine elements in a sequence; the other suffered 'similarity disorder', the inability to substitute one element for another. In a word-association test, if you said 'hut', the first type would produce a string of synonyms, antonyms, and other *substitutions*: 'cabin', 'hovel', 'palace', 'den', 'burrow'. The other type would offer elements which *combine* with 'hut', forming potential sequences: 'burnt out', 'is a poor little house'. Jakobson goes on to point out that the two disorders correspond to two figures of speech—metaphor and metonymy. As the foregoing example shows, 'contiguity disorder' results in substitution in the vertical dimension as in metaphor ('den' for 'hut'), while 'similarity disorder' results in the production of parts of sequences for the wholes as in metonymy ('burnt out' for 'hut'). Jakobson suggested that normal speech behaviour also tends towards one or other extreme, and that literary style expresses itself as a leaning towards either the metaphoric or the metonymic. The historical development from romanticism through realism to symbolism can be understood as an alternation of style from the metaphoric to the metonymic back to the metaphoric. David Lodge, in *The Modes of Modern Writing* (1977), applied the theory to modern literature, adding further stages to a cyclical process: modernism and symbolism are essentially metaphoric, while anti-modernism is realistic and metonymic.

An example. In its broad sense, metonymy involves the shift from one element in a sequence to another, or one element in a context to another: we refer to a *cup* of something (meaning its *contents*); the *turf* (for *racing*), a fleet of a hundred *sails* (for *ships*). Essentially metonymy requires a *context* for its operation; hence Jakobson's linking of realism with metonymy. Realism speaks of its object by offering the reader aspects, parts, and contextual details, in order to evoke a whole. Consider the passage near the opening of Dickens' *Great Expectations*. Pip begins by establishing himself as an identity in a landscape. Reflecting on his orphaned condition, he tells us that he can describe his parents through the only visual remains—their graves: 'As I never saw my father or my mother ... my first fancies regarding what they were like were *unreasonably* [my italics] derived from their tombstones. The shape of the letters on my father's, gave me an odd idea that he was a square stout man .... ' This initial act of identification is metonymic in that Pip links two parts of a context: his father and his father's tombstone. However, this is not a 'realistic' metonymy but an 'unrealistic' derivation, 'an odd idea', although suitably childlike (and in that sense psychologically realistic). Proceeding to the immediate setting on the evening of the convict's appearance, the moment of truth in Pip's life, he gives the following description:

> Ours was the marsh country, down by the river, within, as the river wound, twenty miles of the sea. My first most vivid and broad impression of the *identity of things*,[my italics] seems to me to have been gained on a memorable raw afternoon towards evening. At such a time I found out for certain, that this bleak place overgrown with nettles was the churchyard; and that Philip Pirrip, late of this parish, and also Georgiana wife of the above, were dead and buried; and that ... the dark flat wilderness beyond the churchyard, intersected with dykes and mounds and gates, with scattered cattle feeding on it, was the marshes; and that the low leaden line beyond, was the river; and that the distant savage lair from which the wind was rushing was the sea; and that the small bundle of shivers growing afraid of it all and beginning to cry, was Pip.

Pip's mode of perceiving the 'identity of things' remains metonymic and not metaphoric: churchyard, graves, marshes, river, sea and Pip are conjured up, so to speak, from contextual features. The whole (person, setting) is presented through selected aspects. Pip is evidently more that a 'small bundle of shivers' (he is also a bundle of flesh and bones, thoughts and feelings, social and historical forces), but here his identity is asserted through metonymy, a significant detail offered as his total self at this moment.

In a useful elaboration of Jakobson's theory David Lodge rightly points out that 'context is all-important.' He shows that changing context can change the figures. Here is Lodge's amusing example:

> Those favourite filmic metaphors for sexual intercourse in the pre-permissive cinema, skyrockets and waves pounding on the shore, could be disguised as metonymic background if the consummation were taking place on a beach on Independence Day, but would be perceived as overtly metaphorical if it were taking place on Christmas Eve in a city penthouse.

The example warns us against using Jakobson's theory too inflexibly.

Structuralist poetics: Jonathan Culler

Jonathan Culler made the first attempt to assimilate French structuralism to an Anglo-American critical perspective in 1975. He accepts the premise that linguistics affords the best model of knowledge for the humanities and social sciences. However, he prefers Noam Chomsky's distinction between 'competence' and 'performance' to Saussure's between '*langue*' and '*parole*'. The notion of 'competence' has the advantage of being closely associated with the *speaker* of a language; Chomsky showed that the starting point for an understanding of language was the native speaker's ability to produce and comprehend well-formed sentences on the basis of an unconsciously assimilated knowledge of the language system. Culler brings out the significance of this perspective for literary theory: 'the real object of poetics is not the work itself but its intelligibility. One must attempt to explain how it is that works can be understood; the implicit knowledge, the conventions that enable readers to makes sense of them, must be formulated . . . .' His main endeavour is to shift the focus from the text to the reader (see chapter 5). He believes that we can determine the rules that govern the interpretation of texts, but not those rules that govern the writing of texts. If we begin by establishing a range of interpretations which seem acceptable to skilled readers, we can then establish what norms and procedures led to the interpretations. To put it simply, skilled readers, when faced with a text, seem to know how to make sense of it—to decide what is a possible interpretation and what is not. There seem to be rules governing the sort of sense one might make of the most apparently bizarre literary text. Culler sees the structure not in the system underlying the text but in the system underlying the reader's act of interpretation. To take a bizarre example, here is a three-line poem:

Night is generally my time for walking;
It was the best of times, it was the worst of times;
Concerning the exact year there is no need to be precise.

When I asked a number of colleagues to read it, a variety of interpretative moves were brought into play. One saw a *thematic* link between the lines ('Night', 'time', 'times', 'year'); another tried to envisage a *situation* (psychological or external); another tried to see the poem in terms of formal patternings (a past tense—'was'—framed by present tenses—'is'); another saw the lines as adopting three different attitudes to time: specific, contradictory, and non-specific. One colleague recognised that line two comes from the opening of Dickens' *A Tale of Two Cities*, but still accepted it as a 'quotation' which served a function within the poem. I finally had to reveal that the other lines were also from the openings of Dickens novels (*The Old Curiosity Shop* and *Our Mutual Friend*). What is significant from a Cullerian point of view is not that the readers were caught out but that they followed recognisable procedures for making sense of the lines. I should add that one colleague proved too canny: 'Aren't these lines from novels?'

The main difficulty about Culler's approach surrounds the question of how systematic one can be about the interpretative rules used by readers. He recognises that the procedures of skilled readers will vary with genre and period, but does not allow for the profound ideological differences between readers which may undermine the institutional pressures for conformity in reading practices. It is hard to conceive of a single matrix of rules and conventions which would account for the diversity of interpretations which might be produced in a single period about individual texts. At any rate, we cannot simply take for granted the existence of any entity called a skilled reader, defined as the product of the institutions we call 'literary criticism'.

Structuralism has attracted some literary critics because it promises to introduce a certain rigour and objectivity into the delicate realm of literature. This rigour is achieved at a cost. By subordinating *parole* to *langue* the structuralist neglects the specificity of actual texts, and treats them as if they were like the patterns of iron filings produced by an invisible force. Not only the text but also the author is cancelled as the structuralist places in brackets the actual work and the person who wrote it, in order to isolate the true object of enquiry—the system. In traditional Romantic thought, the author is the thinking and suffering being who precedes the work and whose experience nourishes it; the author is the origin of the text, its creator and progenitor. According to structuralists, writing has no origin. Every individual utterance is preceded by language: in this sense, every text is made up of the 'already written'.

By isolating the system, structuralists also cancel history, since the structures discovered are either universal (the universal structures of the human mind) and therefore timeless, or they are arbitrary segments of a changing and evolving process. Historical questions characteristically are about *change* and *innovation*, whereas structuralism has to exclude them from consideration in order to isolate a system. Therefore structuralists are not interested in the development of the novel or the transition from feudal to Renaissance literary forms, but in the structure of narrative as such and in the system of aesthetics governing a period. Their approach is necessarily static and ahistorical. They are interested therefore in neither the moment of the text's production (its historical context, its formal links with past writing, etc.) nor the moment of its reception (the interpretations imposed on it subsequent to its production).

There is no doubt that structuralism represented a major challenge to the dominant New Critical, Leavisite, and generally humanist types of critical practice. They all presupposed a view of language as something capable of *grasping* reality. Language had been thought of as a reflection of either the writer's mind or the world as seen by the writer. In a sense the writer's language was hardly separable from his or her personality; it expressed the author's very being. However, as we have seen, the Saussurean perspective draws attention to the pre-existence of language. In the beginning was the word, and the word created the text. Instead of saying that an author's language reflects reality, the structuralists argue that the structure of language produces 'reality'. This represents a massive 'demystification' of literature. The source of meaning is no longer the writer's or the reader's *experience* but the operations and oppositions which govern language. Meaning is no longer determined by the individual but by the system which governs the individual.

At the heart of structuralism is a *scientific* ambition to discover the codes, the rules, the systems, which underlie all human social and cultural practices. The disciplines of archaeology and geology are frequently invoked as the models of structuralist enterprise. What we see on the surface are the traces of a deeper history; only by excavating beneath the surface will we discover the geological strata or the ground plans which provide the true explanations for what we see above. One can argue that all science is structuralist in this respect: we see the sun move across the sky, but science discovers the true structure of the heavenly bodies' motion (although one can't help asking with George Moore of Stoppard's *Jumpers* 'What would it have looked like if it had looked as if the earth was rotating?')

Readers who already have some knowledge of the subject will recognise that I have, for tactical reasons, presented only a certain classical type of structuralism in this chapter. Its proponents suggest that definite sets of relations (oppositions, sequences of functions or propositions, syntactical rules) underlie particular practices, and that individual performances derive from structures in the same way as the shape of landscapes derives from the geological strata beneath. A structure is like a centre or point of origin, and replaces other such centres of origins (the individual or history). However, my discussion of Genette showed that the very definition of an opposition within narrative discourse sets up a *play* of meaning which resists a settled or fixed structuration. For example, the opposition between 'description' and 'narration' tends to encourage a 'privileging' of the second term ('description' is ancillary to 'narration'; narrators describe incidentally, as they narrate). But, if we interrogate this now hierarchised pair of terms, we can easily begin to reverse it by showing that 'description' is after all dominant because all narration implies description. In this way we begin to undo the structure which had been centred upon 'narration'. This process of 'deconstruction' which can be set in motion at the very heart of structuralism is one of the major elements in what we call post-structuralism.

Selected Reading

Basic Texts

Barthes, Roland,	*Elements of Semiology*, trans. A. Lavers and C. Smith (Jonathan Cape, London, 1967).
Barthes, Roland,	*Writing Degree Zero*, trans. A. Lavers and C. Smith (Jonathan Cape, London, 1967).
Barthes, Roland,	*Critical Essays*, trans. R. Howard (Northwestern University Press, Evanston, Illinois, 1972).
de Saussure, Ferdinand,	*Course in General Linguistics*, trans. W. Baskin (Fontana/Collins, London, 1974).
Ehrmann, Jacques (ed.),	*Structuralism* (Doubleday, Anchor Books, New York, 1970).
Genette, Gérard,	*Narrative Discourse* (Blackwell, Oxford, 1980).
Genette, Gérard,	*Figures of Literary Discourse*, trans. A. Sheridan (Blackwell, Oxford, 1982), esp. chap 7, 'Frontiers of narrative'.
Jakobson, Roman,	'Linguistics and poetics', in *Style in Language*, ed. T. Sebeok (MIT Press, Cambridge, Mass., 1960), pp. 350–77.
Jakobson, Roman, (with M. Halle),	*Fundamentals of Language* (Mouton, The Hague and Paris, 1975).
Lane, Michael (ed.),	*Structuralism: A Reader* (Jonathan Cape, London, 1970).
Lévi-Strauss, Claude,	*Structural Anthropology*, trans. C. Jacobson and B.G. Schoepf (Allen Lane, London, 1968), esp. chaps 2 and 11.
Lodge, David,	*The Modes of Modern Writing: Metaphor, Metonymy, and the Typology of Modern Literature* (Arnold, London, 1977).
Propp, Vladimir,	*The Morphology of the Folktale* (Texas University Press, Austin and London, 1968).
Todorov, Tzvetan,	*The Fantastic: a Structural Approach to a Literary Genre*, trans. R. Howard

(Cornell University Press, Ithaca, 1975).

Introductions

Culler, Jonathan — *Structuralist Poetics: Structuralism, Linguistics and the Study of Literature* (Routledge & Kegan Paul, London, 1975).

Hawkes, Terence, — *Structuralism and Semiotics* (Methuen, London, 1977).

Robey, David (ed.), — *Structuralism: an Introduction* (Clarendon Press, Oxford, 1973).

Scholes, Robert, — *Structuralism in Literature: An Introduction* (Yale University Press, New Haven and London, 1974).

Todorov, Tzvetan, — *Introduction to Poetics*, trans. R. Howard (The Harvester Press, Brighton, 1981).

Further Reading

Doubrovsky, Serge, — *The New Criticism in France*, trans. D. Coltman (University of Chicago Press, Chicago and London, 1973).

Heath, Stephen, — *The Nouveau Roman: a Study in the Practice of Writing* (Elek, London, 1972), chap. 1.

Jameson, Fredric, — *The Prison-House of Language: A Critical Account of Structuralism and Russian Formalism* (Princeton University Press, Princeton and London, 1972).

CHAPTER FOUR

POST-STRUCTURALIST THEORIES

At some point in the late 1960s, structuralism gave birth to 'post-structuralism'. Some commentators believe that the later developments were already inherent in the earlier phase. One might say that post-structuralism is simply a fuller working-out of the implications of structuralism. But this formulation is not quite satisfactory, because it is evident that post-structuralism tries to deflate the scientific pretensions of structuralism. If structuralism was heroic in its desire to master the world of man-made signs, post-structuralism is comic and anti-heroic in its refusal to take such claims seriously. However, the post-structuralist mockery of structuralism is almost a self mockery: post-structuralists are structuralists who suddenly see the error of their ways.

It is possible to see the beginnings of a post-structuralist counter-movement even in Saussure's linguistic theory. As we have seen, *langue* is the systematic aspect of language which works as the underpinning structure of *parole*, the individual instance of speech or writing. The sign is also bipartite: signifier and signified are like two sides of a coin. However, Saussure also notices that there is no necessary connection between signifier and signified. Sometimes a language will have one word (signifier) for two concepts (signifieds): in English 'sheep' is the animal and 'mutton' the meat; French has only one word for both signifieds ('mouton'). It is as though the various languages carve up the world of things and ideas into different concepts (signifieds) on the one hand, and different words (signifiers) on the other. As Saussure puts it, 'A linguistic system is a series of differences of sound combined with a series of differences of ideas.' The signifier 'hot' is able to work as part of a sign because it *differs* from 'hat', 'hit', 'hop', 'hog', 'lot', and so on. These 'differences' can be aligned with different signifieds.

He concludes with his celebrated remark 'In language there are only differences *without positive terms.*' However, before we jump to the wrong conclusion, he immediately adds that this is only true if we take signifiers and signifieds separately. There is a natural tendency, he assures us, for one signified to seek its own signifier, and to form with it a *positive unit.* Saussure's assertion of a certain stability in signification is natural in a 'pre-Freudian' thinker: while the signifier/signified relationship is arbitrary, speakers in practice require particular signifiers to be securely attached to particular concepts, and therefore they assume that signifier and signified form a unified whole and preserve a certain identity of meaning.

Post-structuralist thought has discovered the essentially *unstable* nature of signification. The sign is not so much a unit with two sides, as a momentary 'fix' between two moving layers. Saussure had recognised that signifier and signified are two separate systems, but he did not see how unstable units of meaning can be when the systems come together. Having established language as a total system independent of physical reality, he tried to retain a sense of the sign's coherence, even though his splitting of the sign into two parts threatened to undo it. Post-structuralists have in various ways prised apart the two halves of the sign.

Surely, we might ask, the unity of the sign is confirmed whenever we use a dictionary to find a meaning (signified) of a word (signifier)? In fact, the dictionary confirms only the relentless deferment of meaning: not only do we find for every signifier several signifieds (a 'crib' signifies a manger, a child's bed, a hut, a job, a mine-shaft lining, a plagiarism, a literal translation, discarded cards at cribbage), but each of the signifieds becomes yet another signifier which can be traced in the dictionary with its own array of signifieds ('bed' signifies a place for sleeping, a garden plot, a layer of oysters, channel of a river, a stratum). The process continues interminably, as the signifiers lead a chameleon-like existence, changing their colours with each new context. Much of the energy of post-structuralism has gone into tracing the insistent activity of the signifier as it forms chains and cross-currents of meaning with other signifiers and defies the orderly requirements of the signified.

Roland Barthes: the plural text

Barthes was undoubtedly the most entertaining, witty, and daring of the French theorists of the 1960s and 1970s. His career took several turns, but preserved a central theme: the conventionality of all forms of representation. He defines literature (in an early essay) as 'a message of the signification of things and not their meaning (by "signification" I refer to the process which produces the meaning and not this meaning itself)'. He echoes Roman Jakobson's definition of the 'poetic' as the 'set to the message', but Barthes stresses the *process* of signification, which appears less and less predictable as his work proceeds. The worst sin a writer can commit is to pretend that language is a natural, transparent medium through which the reader grasps a solid and unified 'truth' or 'reality'. The virtuous writer recognises the artifice of all writing and proceeds to make play with it. Bourgeois ideology, Barthes' *bête noire*, promotes the sinful view that reading is natural and language transparent; it insists on regarding the signifier as the sober partner of the signified, thus in authoritarian manner repressing all discourse into a meaning. Avant-garde writers allow the unconscious of language to rise to the surface: they allow the signifiers to generate meaning at will and to undermine the censorship of the signified and its repressive insistence on one meaning.

If anything marks a post-structuralist phase in Barthes it is his abandoning of scientific aspirations. In *Elements of Semiology* (1967), he believed that structuralist method could explain all the sign-systems of human culture. However, in the very same text, he recognised that structuralist discourse itself could become the object of explanation. The semiological investigator regards his or her own language as a 'second-order' discourse which operates in Olympian fashion upon the 'first-order' object-language. The second-order language is called a metalanguage. In realising that any metalanguage could be put in the position of a first-order language and be interrogated by another metalanguage, Barthes glimpsed an infinite regress (an 'aporia'), which destroys the authority of all metalanguages. This means that, when we read as critics, we can never step outside discourse and adopt a position invulnerable to a subsequent interrogative reading. All discourses, including critical interpretations, are equally *fictive*; none stand apart in the place of Truth.

What might be called Barthes' post-structuralist period is best represented by his short essay 'The death of the author' (1968). He rejects the traditional view that the author is the origin of the text, the source of its meaning, and the only authority for interpretation. At first, this sounds like a restatement of the familiar New-Critical dogma about the literary work's independence (autonomy) from its historical and biographical background. The New Critics believed that the unity of a text lay not in its author's intention but in its structure. This self-contained unity, nevertheless, has subterranean connections with its author, because, in their view, it represents a complex verbal enactment (a 'verbal icon') corresponding to the author's intuitions about the world. Barthes' formula is utterly radical in its dismissal of such humanistic notions. His author is stripped of all metaphysical status and reduced to a location (a cross-road), where language, that infinite storehouse of citations, repetitions, echoes and references, crosses and recrosses. The reader is thus free to enter the text from any direction; there is no correct route. The death of the author is already inherent in structuralism, which treats individual utterances (*paroles*) as the products of impersonal systems (*languages*). What is new in Barthes is the idea that readers are free to open and close the text's signifying process without respect for the signified. They are free to take their pleasure of the text, to follow at will the defiles of the signifier as it slips and slides evading the grasp of the signified. Readers are also sites of language's empire, but they are free to connect the text with systems of meaning and ignore the author's 'intention'.

In *The Pleasure of the Text* (1975) Barthes explores this reckless abandon of the reader. He begins by distinguishing between two senses of 'pleasure':

Pleasure

'pleasure' 'bliss'

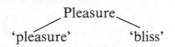

Within Pleasure there is 'bliss' (*jouissance*) and its diluted form, 'pleasure'. The general pleasure of the text is whatever *exceeds* a single transparent meaning. As we read, we see a connection, an echo, or a reference, and this disruption of the text's innocent, linear, flow gives pleasure. Pleasure involves the production of a *join* (seam, fault, or flaw) between two surfaces. The place where naked flesh meets a garment is the focus of erotic pleasure. In texts the effect is to bring something unorthodox or perverse into connection with naked language. Reading the realistic novel we create another 'pleasure' by allowing our attention to wander, or by skipping: 'it is the very rhythm of what is read and what is not read that creates the pleasure of the great narratives.' This is especially true of reading erotic writing (though Barthes insists that pornography has no texts of bliss because it tries too hard to give us the ultimate truth). The more limited reading of pleasure is a comfortable practice which conforms to cultural habits. The text of bliss 'unsettles the reader's historical, cultural, psychological assumptions, ... brings a crisis to his relation with language'. It is clear that such a text does not conform to the sort of easily enjoyed pleasure demanded in the market economy. Indeed, Barthes considers that 'bliss' is very close to boredom: if readers resist the ecstatic collapse of cultural assumptions, they will inevitably find only boredom in the modernist text. How many blissful readers of Joyce's *Finnegans Wake* have there been?

Barthes' *S/Z* (1970) is his most impressive post-structuralist performance. He begins by alluding to the vain ambitions of structuralist narratologists who try 'to see all the world's stories ... within a single structure'. The attempt to uncover *the* structure is vain, because each text possesses a 'difference'. This difference is not a sort of uniqueness, but the result of textuality itself. Each text refers back differently to the infinite sea of the 'already written'. Some writing tries to discourage the reader from freely reconnecting text and this 'already written' by insisting on specific meaning and reference. A realistic novel offers a 'closed' text with a limited meaning. Other texts encourage the reader to *produce* meanings. The 'I' which reads is 'already itself a plurality of other texts' and is allowed by the avant-garde text the maximum liberty to produce meanings by putting what is read in touch with this plurality. The first type of text allows the reader only to be a *consumer* of a fixed meaning, while the second turns the reader into a *producer*. The first type of text is called 'readerly' (*lisible*), the second 'writerly' (*scriptible*). The first is made to be read (consumed), the second to be written (produced). The writerly text exists only in theory, though Barthes' description of it suggests the texts of modernism: 'this ideal text is a galaxy of signifiers, not a structure of signifieds; it has no beginning; . . . we gain access to it by several entrances, none of which can be authoritatively declared to be the main one; the codes it mobilizes extend as far as the eye can reach.'

What are the 'codes'? As the quotation makes clear, they are not the structuralist systems of meaning we might expect. Whatever systems (Marxist, formalist, structuralist, psychoanalytic) we choose to apply to the text can only activate one or more of the virtually infinite 'voices' of the text. As the reader adopts different viewpoints the text's meaning is produced in a multitude of fragments which have no inherent unity. *S/Z* is a reading of Balzac's short novella, *Sarrasine*, which he divides into 561 lexias (reading units). The lexias are read in sequence through the grid of five codes:

Hermeneutic
Semic
Symbolic
Proairetic
Cultural

The hermeneutic code concerns the *enigma* which arises whenever discourse commences. Who is this about? What is happening? What is the obstacle? Who committed the murder? How will the hero's purpose be achieved? A detective story is sometimes called a 'whodunit', thus drawing attention to the special importance of enigma to this genre. In *Sarrasine* the enigma surrounds La Zambinella. Before the question 'Who is she?' is finally answered ('she' is a castrato dressed as a woman), the discourse is spun out with one delaying answer after another: 'she' is a 'woman' ('snare'), 'a creature outside nature' ('ambiguity'), 'no one knows' (a 'jammed answer'). The code of 'semes' concerns the connotations often evoked in characterisation or description. An early account of La Zambinella, for example, sparks off the semes 'femininity', 'wealth', and 'ghostliness'. The symbolic code concerns the polarities and antitheses which allow multivalence and 'reversibility'. It marks out the patterns of sexual and psychoanalytic relations people may enter. For example, when we are introduced to Sarrasine, he is presented in the symbolic relation of 'father and son' ('he was the only son of a lawyer ...'). The absence of the mother (she is unmentioned) is significant, and when the son decides to become an artist he is no longer 'favoured' by the father but 'accursed' (symbolic antithesis). This symbolic coding of the narrative is developed later when we read of the warm-hearted sculptor Bouchardon who enters the absent place of the mother and effects a reconciliation between father and son. The proairetic code (or code of actions) concerns the basic sequential logic of action and behaviour. Barthes marks such a sequence between lexias 95 and 101: the narrator's girl-friend touches the old castrato and reacts by breaking out in a cold sweat; when his relatives react in alarm, she makes for a side room, and throws herself upon a couch in fright. Barthes marks the sequence as five stages of the coded action 'to touch': 1. touching; 2. reaction; 3. general reaction; 4. to flee; 5. to hide. They form a sequence which the reader, unconsciously operating the code, perceives as 'natural' or 'realistic'. Finally, the cultural code embraces all references to the common fund of 'knowledge' (physical, medical, psychological, literary, and so on) produced by society. Sarrasine first reveals his genius 'in one of those works in which future talent struggles with the effervescence of youth' (lexia 174). 'One of those' is a regular formula for signalling this code. Barthes ingeniously notes a double cultural reference: 'Code of ages and code of Art (talent as discipline, youth as effervescence)'.

Why did Barthes choose to study a realistic novella and not an avant-garde text of *jouissance*? The cutting-up of the discourse and the dispersal of its meanings across the musical score of codes seem to deny the text its classic status as realistic story. The novella is exposed as a 'limit text' for realism. The elements of ambivalence destroy the unity of representation which we expect in such writing. The theme of castration, the confusion of sexual roles, and the mysteries surrounding the origins of capitalist wealth all invite an anti-representational reading. It is as if the principles of post-structuralism were already inscribed in this so-called realist text.

Julia Kristeva: language and revolution

Kristeva's most important work on literary meaning is *La révolution du langage poétique* (1974). Unlike that of Barthes her theory is based upon a particular system of ideas: psychoanalysis. The book attempts to explore the process by which what is ordered and rationally accepted is continually being threatened by the 'heterogeneous' and the 'irrational'.

Western thought has for a long time assumed the necessity of a unified 'subject'. To *know* anything presupposes a unified consciousness which does the knowing. Such a consciousness is rather like a focused lens without which nothing can be seen as a distinct object. The medium through which this unified subject perceives objects and truth is *syntax*. An orderly syntax makes for an orderly mind. However, reason has never had things all its own way; it has always been threatened by the subversive noise of pleasure (wine, sex, song), of laughter, and of poetry. Puritan rationalists such as Plato always keep a sharp eye on these dangerous influences. They can all be summed up in the one concept—'desire'. Disruption can go beyond the merely literary to the social level. Poetic language shows how dominant social discourses can be undermined by the creation of new 'subject positions'. This implies that far from being a mere blank which awaits its social or sexual role, the subject is '*in process' and is capable of being other than it is.*

Kristeva gives us a complex psychological account of the relationship between the 'normal' and the 'poetic'. Human beings are from the beginning a space across which physical and psychic impulses flow rhythmically. This indefinite flux of impulses is gradually regulated by the constraints of family and society (potty-training, gender-identification, separation of public and private, and so on). At the earliest, pre-Oedipal stage, the flow of impulses centres on the mother, and does not allow the formulation of a personality but only a rough demarcation of parts of the body and their relations. A disorganised prelinguistic flux of movements, gestures, sounds and rhythms lays a foundation of semiotic material which remains active beneath the mature linguistic performance of the adult. She calls this material 'semiotic' because it works like an unorganised signifying process. We become aware of this activity in dreams in which images are processed in 'illogical' ways (for Freud's theory, see Lacan, below).

In the poetry of Mallarmé and Lautréamont these primary processes of rhythm and sound pattern are liberated from the unconscious (according to Lacan, they *are* the unconscious). Kristeva relates the use of sound in poetry to primary sexual impulses. The opposition *Mama* and *Papa* sets nasal *m* against plosive *p*. The *m* transmits maternal 'orality', while the *p* relates to male 'anality'.

As the semiotic becomes regulated, the beaten pathways become the logic, coherent syntax and rationality of the adult, which Kristeva calls the 'symbolic'. The symbolic works with the substance of the semiotic and achieves a certain mastery over it, but can never produce its own signifying substance. The symbolic places subjects in their positions and makes it possible for them to have identities. Kristeva adopts Lacan's Freudian explanation of the emergence of this phase.

The word 'revolution' in Kristeva's title is not simply metaphoric. The possibility of radical social change is, in her view, bound up with the disruption of authoritarian discourses. Poetic language introduces the subversive openness of the semiotic 'across' society's 'closed' symbolic order: 'What the theory of the unconscious seeks, poetic language practices, within and against the social order.' Sometimes she considers that modernist poetry actually prefigures a social revolution which in the distant future will come about when society has evolved a more complex form. However, at other times she fears that bourgeois ideology will simply recuperate this poetic revolution by treating it as a safety valve for the repressed impulses it denies in society. Kristeva's view of the revolutionary potential of women writers in society is just as ambivalent (see chapter 6).

Jacques Lacan: language and the unconscious

The psychoanalytic writings of Lacan have given critics a new theory of the 'subject'. Marxist, formalist and structuralist critics have dismissed 'subjective' criticisms as Romantic and reactionary, but Lacanian criticism has developed a 'materialist' analysis of the 'speaking subject' which has been more acceptable. According to the linguist Emile Benveniste, 'I', 'he', 'she', and so on, are merely subject positions which language lays down. When I speak, I refer to myself as 'I' and to the person I address as 'you'. When 'you' reply, the persons are reversed and 'I' becomes 'you', and so on. We can communicate only if we accept this strange reversibility of persons. Therefore, the ego which uses the word 'I' is not identical with this 'I'. When I say 'Tomorrow I graduate', the 'I' in the statement is known as the 'subject of the enunciation', and the ego which makes the statement is the 'subject of the enunciating'. Post-structuralist thought enters the gap between these two subjects, while Romantic thought simply elides them.

Lacan considers that human subjects enter a pre-existing system of signifiers which take on meanings only within a language system. The entry into language enables us to find a subject position within a relational system (male/female, father/mother/daughter). This process and the stages which precede it are governed by the unconscious.

According to Freud, during the earliest phases of infanthood the libidinal drives have no definite sexual object but play around the various erotogenic zones of the body (oral, anal, 'phallic'). Before gender or identity are established there is only the rule of the 'pleasure principle'. The 'reality principle' eventually supervenes in the form of the father who threatens the child's Oedipal desire for the mother with the punishment of 'castration'. The repression of desire makes it possible for the male child to identify with the place of the father and with a 'masculine' role. The Oedipal voyage of the female is much less straightforward; Freud's apparent sexism has been attacked by some feminist critics (see Chapter 6). This phase introduces morality, law, and religion, symbolised as 'patriarchal law', and induces the development of a 'superego' in the child. However, the repressed desire does not go away and remains in the unconscious, thus producing a radically *split* subject. Indeed, this force of desire *is* the unconscious.

Lacan's distinction between the 'imaginary' and the 'symbolic' corresponds to Kristeva's between 'semiotic' and 'symbolic'. This 'imaginary' is a state in which there is no clear distinction between subject and object: no central self exists to set object apart from subject. In the prelinguistic 'mirror phase' the child, from within this 'imaginary' state of being, starts to project a certain unity into the fragmented self-image in the mirror (there does not have to be an actual mirror); he or she produces a 'fictional' ideal, an 'ego'. This specular (speculum = mirror) image is still partly imaginary (it is not clear whether it is the child or another), but also partly differentiated as 'another'. The imaginary tendency continues even after the formation of the ego, because the myth of a unified selfhood depends upon this ability to identify with objects in the world as 'others'. Nevertheless, the child must also learn to differentiate itself from others if it is to become a subject in its own right. With the father's prohibition the child is thrown headlong into the 'symbolic' world of differences (male/female, father/son, present/absent, and so on). Indeed, the 'phallus' (not the penis but its 'symbol') is, in Lacan's system, the privileged signifier, which helps all signifiers achieve a unity with their signifieds. In the symbolic domain phallus is king. As we shall see, feminist critics have had a good deal to say about this.

Neither the imaginary nor the symbolic can fully comprehend the Real, which remains out there somewhere beyond their reach. Our instinctive *needs* are shaped by the discourse in which we express our *demand* for satisfaction. However, discourse's moulding of needs leaves not satisfaction but *desire*, which runs on in the chain of signifiers. When 'I' express my desire in words, 'I' am always subverted by that unconscious which presses on with its own sideways game. This unconscious works on in metaphoric and metonymic substitutions and displacements which elude consciousness, but reveals itself in dreams, jokes, and art.

Lacan restates Freud's theories in the language of Saussure. Essentially, unconscious processes are identified with the unstable *signifier*. As we have seen, Saussure's attempts to solder up the gap between the separate systems of signifiers and signifieds was in vain. For example, when a subject enters the symbolic order and accepts a *position* as 'son' or 'daughter', a certain linking of signifier and signified is made possible. However, 'I' am never where I think; 'I' stand at the axis of signifier and signified, a split being, never able to give my position a full presence. In Lacan's version of the sign, the signified 'slides' beneath a signifier which 'floats'. Freud considered dreams the main outlet for repressed desires. His theory of dreams is re-interpreted as a textual theory. The unconscious hides meaning in symbolic images which need to be deciphered. Dream images undergo 'condensation' (several images combine) and 'displacement' (significance shifts from one image to a contiguous one). Lacan calls the first process 'metaphor' and the second 'metonymy' (see Jakobson, chapter 3). In other words, he believes that the garbled and enigmatic dream work follows the laws of the signifier. Freud's 'defence mechanisms' too are treated as figures of speech (irony, ellipsis, and so on). Any kind of psychic distortion is restated as a quirk of the signifier rather than some mysterious prelinguistic urge. For Lacan there never were any undistorted signifiers. His psychoanalysis is the scientific rhetoric of the unconscious.

His Freudianism has encouraged modern criticism to abandon faith in language's power to refer to things and to express ideas or feelings. Modernist literature often resembles dreams in its avoidance of a governing narrative position and its free play of meaning. Lacan himself wrote a much discussed analysis of Poe's 'The Purloined Letter', a story containing two episodes. In the first, the Minister perceives that the Queen is anxious about a letter she has left lying exposed on a table unnoticed by the King who has entered her boudoir unexpectedly. The Minister replaces the letter with a similar one. The Queen cannot intervene for fear that the King will be alerted. In the second episode, following the prefect of police's failure to find the letter in the Minister's house, Dupin (a detective) immediately sees it openly thrust in a card-rack on the Minister's mantlepiece. He returns, distracts the Minister, and replaces the letter with a similar one. Lacan points out that the letter's contents are never revealed. The story's development is shaped not by the character of individuals or the contents of the letter but by the *position* of the letter in relation to the trio of persons in each episode. These relations to the letter are defined by Lacan according to three kinds of 'glance': the first sees nothing (the King's and the prefect's); the second sees that the first glance sees nothing but thinks its secret safe (the Queen's and, in the second episode, the Minister's); the third sees that the first two glances leave the 'hidden' letter exposed (the Minister's and Dupin's). The letter, then, acts like a signifier by producing subject positions for the characters in the narrative. Lacan considers that in this the story illustrates the psychoanalytic theory that the symbolic order is 'constitutive for the subject';

the subject receives a 'decisive orientation' from the 'itinerary of a signifier'. He treats the story as an allegory of psychoanalysis, but also considers psychoanalysis as a model of fiction. The repetition of the structure of scene one in scene two is governed by the effects of a pure signifier (the letter); the characters move into their places as the unconscious prompts.

For a fuller account not only of Lacan's essay but of Derrida's critical reading of Lacan's reading, one should look at Barbara Johnson's excellent essay (in R. Young's *Untying the Text*; see reading list). In a brilliant demonstration of post-structuralist thought she introduces a further displacement of meaning into the potentially endless sequence, Poe > Lacan > Derrida > Johnson.

Jacques Derrida: deconstruction

Derrida's paper 'Structure, Sign, and Play in the Discourse of the Human Sciences', given at a symposium at Johns Hopkins University in 1966, virtually inaugurated a new critical movement in the United States. Its argument put in question the basic metaphysical assumptions of Western philosophy since Plato. The notion of 'structure', he argues, even in 'structuralist' theory has always presupposed a 'centre' of meaning of some sort. This 'centre' governs the structure but is itself not subject to structural analysis (to find the structure of the centre would be to find another centre). People desire a centre because it guarantees *being as presence*. For example, we think of our mental and physical life as centred on an 'I'; this personality is the principle of unity which underlies the structure of all that goes on in this space. Freud's theories completely undermine this metaphysical certainty by revealing a division in the self between conscious and unconscious. Western thought has developed innumerable terms which operate as centering principles: being, essence, substance, truth, form, beginning, end, purpose, consciousness, man, God, and so on. It is important to note that Derrida does not assert the possibility of thinking outside such terms; any attempt to undo a particular concept is to become caught up in the terms which the concept depends on. For example, if we try to undo the centering concept of 'consciousness' by asserting the disruptive counterforce of the 'unconscious', we are in danger of introducing a new centre, because we cannot choose but enter the conceptual system (conscious/unconscious) we are trying to dislodge. All we *can* do is to refuse to allow either pole in a system (body/soul, good/bad, serious/unserious) to become the centre and guarantor of presence.

This desire for a centre is called 'logocentrism' in Derrida's classic work, *On Grammatology*. 'Logos' (Greek for 'word') is a term which in the New Testament carries the greatest possible concentration of presence : 'In the beginning was the Word.' Being the origin of all things, the 'Word' underwrites the full presence of the world; everything is the effect of this one cause. Even though the Bible is written, God's word is essentially *spoken*. A spoken word, emitted from a living body appears to be closer to an originating thought than a written word. Derrida argues that this privileging of speech over writing (he calls it 'phonocentrism') is a classic feature of logocentrism.

What prevents the sign from being a full presence? Derrida invents the term '*différance*' to convey the divided nature of the sign. In French, the 'a' in '*différance*' is not heard, and so we hear only '*differénce*'. The ambiguity is perceptible only in writing: the verb '*différer*' means both 'to differ' and 'to defer'. To 'differ' is a spatial concept; the sign emerges from a system of differences which are spaced out within the system. To 'defer' is temporal: signifiers enforce an endless postponement of 'presence' (as in the dictionary example above). Phonocentric thought ignores '*différance*' and insists upon the self-presence of the spoken word.

Phonocentrism treats writing as a contaminated form of speech. Speech seems nearer to originating thought. When we hear speech we attribute to it a 'presence' which we take to be lacking in writing. The speech of the great actor, orator, or politician is thought to possess 'presence'; it incarnates, so to speak, the speaker's soul. Writing seems relatively impure and obtrudes its own system in physical marks which have a relative permanence; writing can be repeated (printed, reprinted, and so on) and this repetition invites interpretation and re-interpretation. Even when a speech is subjected to interpretation it is usually in written form. Writing does not need the writer's presence, but speech always implies an immediate presence. The sounds made by a speaker evaporate in the air and leave no trace (unless recorded), and therefore do not appear to contaminate the originating thought as in writing. Philosophers have often expressed their dislike of writing; they fear that it will destroy the authority of philosophic Truth. This Truth depends upon pure thought (logic, ideas, propositions) which risk contamination when written. Francis Bacon believed that one of the main obstacles to scientific advance was the love of eloquence: 'men began to hunt more after words that matter; and more after ... tropes and figures, than after the weight of matter, ... soundness of argument.' However, as the word 'eloquence' suggests, the qualities in writing to which he objected are those originally developed by orators. Thus, those very features of elaboration in writing which threaten to cloud the purity of thought were originally cultivated for speech.

This coupling of 'writing' and 'speech' is an example of what Derrida calls a 'violent hierarchy'. Speech has full presence, while writing is secondary and threatens to contaminate speech with its materiality. Western philosophy has supported this ranking in order to preserve presence. But, as the Bacon example shows, the hierarchy can easily be undone and reversed. We begin to see that both speech and writing share certain writerly features: both are signifying processes which lack presence. To complete the reversal of the hierarchy, we can now say that speech is a species of writing. This reversal is the first stage of a Derridean 'deconstruction'.

Derrida uses the term 'supplement' to convey the unstable relationship between couplets such as speech/writing. For Rousseau writing is merely a supplement to speech; it adds something inessential. In French, '*suppléer*' also means 'to substitute' (to take the place of), and Derrida shows that writing not only supplements but also takes the place of speech, because speech is always already written. All human activity involves this supplementarity (addition-substitution). When we say that 'nature' preceded 'civilisation', we are asserting another violent hierarchy in which a pure presence lauds itself over a mere supplement. However, if we look closely, we find that nature is always already contaminated with civilisation; there is no 'original' nature, only a myth which we desire to promote.

Consider another example. Milton's *Paradise Lost* may be said to rest on the distinction between good and evil. Good has the original fullness of being. It originated with God. Evil is a second comer, a supplement, which contaminates his original unity of being. However, if we look more closely, we begin to see reversal taking place. For example, if we seek a time when good was without evil, we find ourselves caught in an abysmal regression. Was it before the Fall? Before Satan's? What caused Satan's fall? Pride. Who created pride? God, who created angels and humans free to sin. We never reach an original moment of pure goodness. We may reverse the hierarchy and say that there are no 'good' acts by humans until after the Fall. Adam's first act of sacrifice is an expression of love for the fallen Eve. This 'goodness' comes only after evil. God's prohibition itself presupposes evil. In *Areopagitica* Milton opposed the licensing of books because he believed that we can be virtuous only if we are given the opportunity to struggle against evil: 'that which purifies us is trial, and trial is by what is contrary.' Thus, good comes *after* evil. There are many critical and theological strategies which can sort out this mess, but there remains a basis for deconstruction. Such a reading begins by noting the hierarchy, proceeds to reverse it, and finally resists the assertion of a new hierarchy by displacing the second term from a position of superiority too. Blake believed that Milton was on Satan's side in his great epic, and Shelley thought that Satan was morally superior to God. They simply reverse the hierarchy, substituting evil for good. A deconstructive reading would go on to recognise that the couplet cannot be hierarchised in either direction without 'violence'. Evil is both addition *and* substitution. Deconstruction can begin when we locate the moment when a text *transgresses the laws it appears to set up for itself*. At this point texts go to pieces, so to speak.

In 'Signature Event Context' Derrida gives writing three characteristics: 1. a written sign is a mark which can be repeated in the absence not only of the subject who emitted it in a specific context but also of a specific addressee; 2. the written sign can break its 'real context' and can be read in a different context regardless of what its writer intended. Any chain of signs can be 'grafted' into a discourse in another context (as in a quotation); 3. the written sign is subject to 'spacing' ('*espacement*') in two senses: first, it is separated from other signs in a particular chain; secondly, it is separated from 'present reference' (that is, it can refer only to something not actually present in it). These characteristics appear to distinguish writing from speech. Writing involves a certain irresponsibility, because if signs are repeatable out of context, then what authority can they possess? Derrida proceeds to deconstruct the hierarchy by, for example, pointing out that when we interpret oral signs, we have to recognise certain stable and identical forms (signifiers), whatever accent, tone, or distortion may be involved in the utterance. It appears that we have to exclude the accidental phonic (sound) substance and recover a pure form. This form is the repeatable signifier, which we had thought characteristic of writing. Once again, we conclude that speech is a species of writing.

J.L. Austin's theory of 'speech acts' was developed to supersede the old logical-positivist view of language which assumed that the only meaningful statements are those which describe a state of affairs in the world. All other sorts of statements are not real ones but 'pseudo-statements'. Austin uses the term 'constative' to cover the first (referential statements), and 'performative' to cover those utterances which actually perform the actions they describe ('I swear to tell the whole truth and nothing but the truth' *performs* an oath). Derrida acknowledges that this makes a break with logocentric thought by recognising that speech does not have to represent something to have a meaning. However, Austin also distinguishes between degrees of linguistic force. To make a merely linguistic utterance (say, to speak an English sentence) is a *locutionary* act. A speech act which has *illocutionary* force involves performing the act (to promise, to swear, to argue, to affirm, and so on). A speech act has *perlocutionary* force if it brings about an effect (I *persuade* you by arguing; I *convince* you by swearing; and so on). Austin requires that speech acts must have contexts. An oath can occur only in a court within the appropriate judicial framework or in other situations in which oaths are conventionally performed. Derrida questions this by suggesting that the repeatability ('iterability') of the speech act is more fundamental than its attachment to a context.

Austin remarks in passing that to be performative a statement must be spoken 'seriously' and not be a joke or used in a play or poem. An oath in a Hollywood court scene is 'parasitic' upon a real-life oath. John Searle's reply to Derrida, 'Reiterating the differences', defends Austin's view and argues that a 'serious' discourse is logically prior to fictional, 'parasitic' citations of it. Derrida probes this and neatly demonstrates that a 'serious' performative cannot occur unless it is a repeatable sign-sequence (what Barthes called the 'always-already-written'). A real courtroom oath is just a special case of the game people play in films and books. What Austin's pure performative and the impure, parasitic versions have in common is that they involve repetition and citation, which are typical of the 'written'.

Since his 1966 paper Derrida has become an academic celebrity in the United States. Deconstruction has been taken up widely in humanities departments, and Derrida has a teaching position at Yale University.

The power of the deconstructive movement can be gauged by the fact that many other major intellectual traditions have been forced into radical reassessments. For example, a *rapprochement* between deconstructive philosophy and modern Marxism is impressively undertaken by Michael Ryan in his *Marxism and Deconstruction* (1982), in which he shows how both have encouraged 'plurality' rather than 'authoritarian unity', criticism rather than obedience, 'difference' rather than 'identity', and a general scepticism about absolute or totalising systems.

American deconstruction

American critics flirted with a number of alien presences in their attempts to throw off the long-cherished formalism of the New Critics. The scientific 'myth criticism' of Northrop Frye, the Hegelian Marxism of Lukács, the phenomenology of Poulet, and the rigours of French structuralism each had its day. It is something of a surprise that Derrida won over many of America's most powerful critics. Several of them are Romantic specialists. Romantic poets are intensely concerned with experiences of timeless illumination ('epiphanies') which occur at certain privileged moments in their lives. They try to recapture these 'spots of time' in their poetry, and to saturate their words with this absolute presence. However, they also lament the loss of 'presence': 'there hath passed away a glory from the earth'. It is not therefore surprising that Paul de Man and others have found Romantic poetry an open invitation to deconstruction. Indeed de Man argues that the Romantics actually deconstruct their own writing by showing that the presence they desire is always absent, always in the past or future.

De Man's *Blindness and Insight* (1971) and *Allegories of Reading* (1979) are impressively rigorous works of deconstruction. Their debt to Derrida is evident, but de Man develops his own terminology. The first book circles around the paradox that critics only achieve insight through a certain blindness. They adopt a method or theory which is quite at odds with the insights it produces: 'All these critics [Lukács, Blanchot, Poulet] seem curiously doomed to say something different from what they meant to say.' The insights could be gained only because the critics were 'In the grip of this peculiar blindness'. For example, the American New Critics based their practice upon the Coleridgean notion of organic form, according to which a poem has a formal unity analogous to that of natural form. However, instead of discovering in poetry the unity and coherence of the natural world, they reveal multi-faceted and ambiguous meanings: 'This unitarian criticism finally becomes a criticism of ambiguity.' This ambiguous poetic language seems to contradict their idea of an object-like totality.

De Man believes that this insight-in-blindness is facilitated by an unconscious slide from one kind of unity to another. The unity which the New Critics so frequently discover is not in the text but in the act of interpretation. Their desire for total understanding initiates the 'hermeneutic circle' of interpretation. Each element in a text is understood in terms of the whole, and the whole is understood as a totality made up of all the elements. This interpretive movement is part of a complex process which produces literary 'form'. Mistaking this 'circle' of interpretation for the text's unity helps them sustain a blindness which produces insight into poetry's divided and multiple meaning (the elements do not form a unity). Criticism must be ignorant of the insight it produces.

Derrida's questioning of the distinction between speech and writing is paralleled by his interrogation of those between 'philosophy' and 'literature', and between the 'literal' and the 'figurative'. Philosophy can only be philosophical if it ignores or denies its own textuality: it believes it stands at a remove from such contamination. 'Literature' is regarded by philosophy as mere fiction, as a discourse in the grip of 'figures of speech'. By reversing the hierarchy philosophy/literature Derrida places philosophy 'under erasure' (~~philosophy~~): philosophy is itself governed by rhetoric and yet is preserved as a distinct form of 'writing' (we still see 'philosophy' under the mark of erasure). Reading philosophy as literature does not prevent us from reading literature as philosophy; Derrida refuses to assert a new hierarchy (literature/philosophy), although some Derrideans are guilty of this partial deconstruction. Similarly, we discover that 'literal' language is in fact 'figurative' language whose figuration has been forgotten. However, the concept of the 'literal' is not thereby eliminated but only deconstructed. It remains in effect, but 'under erasure'.

In *Allegories of Reading* de Man develops a 'rhetorical' type of deconstruction already begun in *Blindness and Insight*. 'Rhetoric' is the classical term for the art of persuasion. De Man is concerned with the theory of 'tropes' which accompanies rhetorical treatises. 'Figures of speech' (tropes) allow writers to say one thing but mean something else: to substitute one sign for another (metaphor), to displace meaning from one sign in a chain to another (metonymy), and so on. Tropes pervade language, exerting a force which destabilises logic, and thereby denies the possibility of a straightforwardly literal or referential use of language. To the question 'Tea or coffee?' I reply 'What's the difference?' My rhetorical question (meaning 'It makes no difference which I choose') contradicts the logic of my question's 'literal' meaning ('What is the difference between tea and coffee?'). De Man shows that, just as critical insights result from critical blindness, so passages of explicit critical reflection or thematic statement in literary texts seem to depend on the suppression of the implications of the rhetoric used in such passages. De Man grounds his theory in close readings of specific texts, and considers that it is the effects of language and rhetoric that prevent a direct representation of the real. He follows Nietzsche in believing that language is essentially figurative and not referential or expressive; there is no original unrhetorical language. This means that 'reference' is always contaminated with figurality. He adds (we cannot elaborate here) that 'grammar' is the third term which nudges referential meaning into figurative form.

De Man applies these arguments to criticism itself. Reading is always necessarily 'misreading', because 'tropes' inevitably intervene between critical and literary texts. Critical writing conforms essentially to the literary figure we call 'allegory'; it is a sequence of signs which stands at a distance from another sequence of signs, and seeks to stand in its place. Criticism is thus returned, like philosophy, to the common textuality of 'literature'. What is the point of this 'misreading'? De Man thinks that some misreadings are correct and others incorrect. A correct misreading tries to contain and not repress the inevitable misreadings which all language produces. At the centre of this argument is the belief that literary texts are *self-deconstructing*: 'a literary text simultaneously asserts and denies the authority of its own rhetorical mode.' The deconstructor appears to have little to do except to collude with the text's own processes. If he or she succeeds, a correct misreading can be achieved.

De Man's refined critical procedure does not involve an actual denial of language's referential function (reference is merely placed 'under erasure'). However, since texts never seem to emerge from their textuality, there may be something in Terry Eagleton's view that American (and especially de Man's) deconstruction perpetuates by another means New Criticism's dissolution of history. While the New Critics cocooned the text in 'form' to protect it from history, the deconstructors swallow up history in an expanded empire of literature, 'viewing famines, revolutions, soccer matches and sherry trifle as yet more undecidable "text"'. Deconstruction cannot in theory establish a hierarchy text/history, but in practice it sees only text as far as the eye can reach.

The rhetorical type of post-structuralism has taken various forms. In historiography (the theory of history) Hayden White has attempted a radical deconstruction of the writings of well-known historians. In *Tropics of Discourse* (1978) he argues that historians believe their narratives to be objective, but because it involves structure their narration cannot escape textuality: 'Our discourse always tends to slip away from our data towards the structures of consciousness with which we are trying to grasp them.' Whenever a new discipline arises it must establish the adequacy of its own language to the objects in its field of study. However, this is done not by logical argument but by a '*pre*figurative move that is more tropical than logical'. When a historian orders the material of his study, he renders it manageable by the silent application of what Kenneth Burke called the 'Four Master Tropes': metaphor, metonymy, synecdoche, and irony. Historical thinking is not possible except in terms of tropes. White agrees with Piaget in thinking that this figurative consciousness may be part of normal psychological development. He goes on to examine the writings of major thinkers (Freud, Marx, E.P. Thompson, and others) and shows that their 'objective knowledge' or 'concrete historical reality' is always shaped by the master tropes.

In literary criticism Harold Bloom has made spectacular use of tropes. Despite being a Yale professor, he is less radically 'textual' than de Man or Hartman, and still treats literature as a special field of study. However, his combination of the theory of tropes, Freudian psychology and cabbalistic mysticism is a daring one. He argues that since Milton, the first truly 'subjective' poet, poets have suffered an awareness of their 'belatedness': coming late in poetic history they fear that their poetic fathers have already used up all the available inspiration. They experience an Oedipal hatred of the father, a desperate desire to deny paternity. The suppression of their aggressive feelings gives rise to various defensive strategies. No poem stands on its own, but always in relation to another. In order to write belatedly, poets must enter a psychic struggle to create an imaginative space. This involves 'misreading' their masters in order to produce a new interpretation. This 'poetic misprision' creates the required space in which they can communicate their own authentic inspiration. Without this aggressive wrenching of predecessors' meaning, tradition would stifle all creativity.

Cabbalistic writings (Jewish rabbinical texts which reveal hidden meanings in the Bible) are classic examples of *revisionary* texts. Bloom believes that Isaac Luria's sixteenth-century version of cabbalistic mysticism is an exemplary model of the way poets revise earlier poets in post-Renaissance poetry. He develops from Luria the three stages of revision: *limitation* (taking a new look), *substitution* (replacing one form by another), and *representation* (restoring a meaning). When a 'strong' poet writes, he repeatedly passes through the three stages in a dialectical manner, as he grapples with the strong poets of the past (I intentionally leave Bloom's masculine idiom exposed).

In *A Map of Misreading* (1975) he charts how meaning is produced in 'Post-Enlightenment images, by the language strong poets use in defence against, and response to, the language of prior strong poets'. The 'tropes' and 'defenses' are interchangeable forms of 'revisionary ratios'. Strong poets cope with the 'anxiety of influence' by adopting separately or successively six psychic defences. These appear in their poetry as tropes which allow a poet to 'swerve' from a father's poems. The six tropes are irony, synecdoche, metonymy, hyperbole/litotes, metaphor, and metalepsis. Bloom uses six classical words to describe the six kinds of relationship between the texts of fathers and sons (revisionary ratios): *clinamen, tessera, kenosis, daemonisation, askesis,* and *apophrades. Clinamen* is the 'swerve' a poet makes in order to justify a new poetic direction (a direction which, it is implied, the master would or should have taken). This involves a deliberate misinterpretation of an earlier poet. *Tessera* is 'fragment': a poet treats the materials of a precursor poem as if they were in pieces, and required the finishing touch of the successor. *Clinamen* (revisionary ratio) has the rhetorical form of 'irony' (the figure of speech, not of thought), and is the psychic defence called 'reaction-formation'. Irony says one thing and means something different (sometimes the opposite). The other ratios are similarly expressed as both trope and psychic defence (*tessera* = synecdoche = 'turning against the Self', and so on). Unlike de Man and White, Bloom does not privilege rhetoric in his readings. It would be more accurate to call his method 'psychocritical'.

Bloom pays particular attention to the Romantic 'crisis-poems' of Wordsworth, Shelley, Keats and Tennyson. Each poet struggles to creatively misread his predecessors. Each poem passes through the stages of revision and each stage works through the pairs of revisionary ratios. Shelley's 'Ode to the West Wind', for example, struggles with Wordsworth's 'Immortality' ode as follows: stanzas I—II, *clinamen/tessera*; IV, *kenosis/daemonisation*; *V, askesis/apophrades*. It is necessary to study Part III of *A Map of Misreading* to grasp the full working of Bloom's method.

Geoffrey Hartman, having emerged from New Criticism, plunged into deconstruction with gay abandon and left in his wake a recklessly scattered trail of fragmentary texts (collected in *Beyond Formalism*, 1970, *The Fate of Reading*, 1975, and *Criticism in the Wilderness*, 1980). Like de Man he regards criticism as inside rather than outside literature. He has used this licence to justify his seemingly random pillaging of other texts (literary, philosophical, popular) to spin out his own discourse. For example, at one point he writes about the harshness and strangeness of Christ's parables, which were smoothed over by the 'older hermeneutics' which 'tended to be incorporative or reconciling, like Donne's "spider love that transubstantiates all"'. Donne's phrase is drawn in by association. 'Transubstantiation' is used metaphorically in a poem about love, but Hartman activates its religous connotations; his 'incorporative' picks up the incarnational connotations of 'transubstantiation'. He randomly suppresses or ignores the poisonous implication (in Donne's period) of 'spider'. His critical writings are frequently interrupted and complicated by such imperfectly digested references. The imperfection reflects Hartman's view that critical reading should not aim to produce consistent meaning but to reveal 'contradictions and equivocations' in order to make fiction 'interpretable by making it less readable'. Since criticism is inside literature, it must be equally unreadable.

He rebels against the scholarly common-sense criticism of the Arnoldian tradition ('sweetness and light'). More generally he adopts a post-structuralist rejection of science's 'ambition to master ... its subject (text, psyche) by technocratic, predictive, authoritarian formulas'. However, he also questions the speculative and abstract 'sky-flying' of the philosopher-critic, who flies too high to keep in touch with actual texts. His own brand of mildly speculative and densely textual criticism is an attempt at reconciliation. He both admires and fears Derrida's radical theory. He welcomes criticism's newly-found creativity, but hesitates before the yawning abyss of indeterminacy, which threatens it with chaos. As Vincent Leitch has written, 'he emerges as a voyeur of the border, who watches or imagines crossover and warns of dangers'. And yet, one cannot help thinking that Hartman's philosophical doubts are lulled by the lure of textual pleasure. Consider the following extract from his discussion of Derrida's *Glas*, which incorporates passages from Genet's *Journal du voleur (The Thief's Journal)*:

> ***Glas*, then, is Derrida's own *Journal du voleur*, and reveals the vol-onto-theology of writing. Writing is always theft or bricolage of the logos. The theft redistributes the logos by a new principle of equity ... as the volatile seed of flowers. Property, even in the form of the *nom propre*, is *non-propre*, and writing is an act of crossing the line of the text, of making it indeterminate, or revealing the *midi* as the *mi-dit*.**

During the sixties J. Hillis Miller was deeply influenced by the Geneva School's 'phenomenological' criticism (see chapter 5). His work since 1970 has centred on the deconstruction of fiction (especially in *Fiction and Repetition: Seven English Novels*, 1982). This phase was inaugurated with a fine paper on Dickens given in 1970, in which he takes up Jakobson's theory of metaphor and metonymy (see chapter 3). He begins by showing how the realism of *Sketches by Boz* is not a mimetic effect but a figurative one. Looking at Monmouth Street, Boz sees 'things, human artifacts, streets, buildings, vehicles, old clothes in shops'. These things metonymically signify something which is absent: he infers from the things 'the life that is lived among them'. However, Miller's account does not end with this relatively structuralist analysis of realism. He shows how the metonymic dead men's clothes come to life in Boz's mind as he imagines their absent wearers: 'waistcoats have almost burst with anxiety to put themselves on'. This metonymic 'reciprocity' between a person and his surroundings (house, possessions, and so on) 'is the basis for the metaphorical substitutions so frequent in Dickens' fiction'. Metonymy asserts an *association* between clothes and wearer, while metaphor suggests a *similarity* between them. First, clothes and wearer are linked by context, and secondly, as context fades, we allow clothes to substitute for wearer. Miller perceives a further self-conscious fictionality in Dickens' fondness for theatrical metaphor. He frequently describes the behaviour of individuals as an imitation of theatrical styles or of works of art (one character goes through 'an admirable bit of serious pantomime', speaks in 'a stage whisper', and appears later 'like the ghost of Queen Anne in the tent scene in Richard'). There is an endless deferment of presence: everyone imitates or repeats someone else's behaviour, real or fictional. The metonymic process encourages a literal reading (this *is* London), while at the same time it acknowledges its own figurality. We discover that metonymy is as much a fiction as metaphor. Miller in effect deconstructs Jakobson's original opposition between 'realistic' metonymy and 'poetic' metaphor. A 'correct interpretation' of them sees the 'figurative as figurative'. Both 'invite misinterpretation which takes as substantial what are in fact only linguistic fictions'. Poetry, however metaphorical, is liable to be 'read literally', and realistic writing, however metonymic, is open to 'a correct figurative reading which sees it as fiction rather than *mimesis*'. It can be argued that Miller here falls into the vice of incomplete reversal of a metaphysical hierarchy (literal/figurative). By talking about a 'correct interpretation' and a 'misinterpretation' he exposes himself to the anti-deconstructive arguments of Gerald Graff (*Literature Against Itself*, 1979), who objects that Miller 'forecloses the very possibility of language's referring to the world' and therefore implies that every text (not just Dickens') calls its own assumptions into question.

Barbara Johnson's *The Critical Difference* (1980) contains subtle and lucid deconstructive readings of literature and criticism. She shows that both literary and critical texts set up 'a network of differences into which the reader is lured with a promise of comprehension.' For example, in *S/Z* Barthes identifies and dismantles the masculine/feminine 'difference' in Balzac's *Sarrasine* (see above). By cutting up the novella into lexias Barthes appears to resist any total reading of the text's meaning in terms of sexuality. Johnson shows that Barthes' reading nevertheless privileges 'castration', and, further, that his distinction between the 'readerly' and the 'writerly' text corresponds to Balzac's distinction between the ideal woman (Zambinella as conceived by Sarrasine) and the castrato (Zambinella in actuality). Thus Zambinella resembles both the perfect unity of the readerly text and the fragmented and undecidable writerly text. Barthes' method of reading evidently favours 'castration' (cutting up). Sarrasine's image of Zambinella is based upon narcissism: her perfection (perfect woman) is the symmetrical counterpart of Sarrasine's masculine self-image. That is, Sarrasine loves 'the image of the lack of what he thinks he himself possesses.' Oddly enough, the castrato is 'simultaneously outside the difference between the sexes as well as representing the literalization of its illusory symmetry.' In this way Zambinella destroys Sarrasine's reassuring masculinity by showing that it is based on castration.

Johnson's essential point about Barthes' reading of Balzac is that Barthes actually spells out the fact of castration where Balzac leaves it unspoken. In this way Barthes reduces a 'difference' to an 'identity'. Johnson makes this point not as a criticism of Barthes but as an illustration of the inevitable blindness of critical insight (to use de Man's terms).

Discourse and power: Michel Foucault and Edward Saïd

There is another strand in post-structuralist thought which believes that the world is more than a galaxy of texts, and that some theories of textuality ignore the fact that discourse is involved in *power*. They reduce political and economic forces, and ideological and social control, to aspects of signifying processes. When a Hitler or a Stalin seems to dictate to an entire nation by wielding the power of discourse, it is absurd to treat the effect as simply occurring within discourse. It is evident that real power is exercised through discourse, and that this power has real effects.

The father of this line of thought is the German philosopher Nietzsche, who said that people first decide what they want and then fit the facts to their aim: 'Ultimately, man finds in things nothing but what he himself has imported into them.' All knowledge is an expression of the 'Will to Power'. This means that we cannot speak of any absolute truths or of objective knowledge. People recognise a particular piece of philosophy or scientific theory as 'true' only if it fits the descriptions of truth laid down by the intellectual or political authorities of the day, by the members of the ruling élite, or by the prevailing ideologues of knowledge.

Like other post-structuralists Foucault regards discourse as a central human activity, but not as a universal, 'general text', a vast sea of signification. He is interested in the historical dimension of discursive *change*. What it is possible to say will change from one era to another. In science a theory is not recognised in its own period if it does not conform to the power consensus of the institutions and official organs of science. Mendel's genetic theories fell on deaf ears in the 1860s; they were promulgated in a 'void' and had to wait until the twentieth century for acceptance. It is not enough to speak the truth; one must be 'in the truth'.

In his early work on 'madness' Foucault found it difficult to find examples of 'mad' discourse (except in literature: de Sade, Artaud). He deduced that the rules and procedures which determine what is considered normal or rational successfully silence what they exclude. Individuals working within particular discursive practices cannot think or speak without obeying the unspoken 'archive' of rules and constraints; otherwise they risk being condemned to madness or silence. This discursive mastery works not just by exclusion, but also by 'rarefaction' (each practice narrows its content and meaning by thinking only in terms of 'author' and 'discipline'). Finally, there are the social constraints, especially the formative power of the education system, which defines what is rational and scholarly.

Foucault's books, especially *Madness and Civilization* (1961). *The Birth of the Clinic* (1963), *The Order of Things* (1966), *Discipline and Punish* (1975), and *The History of Sexuality* (1976), show that various forms of 'knowledge' about sex, crime, psychiatry, and medicine have arisen and been replaced. He concentrates on the fundamental shifts occurring between epochs. He offers no period generalisations, but traces the overlapping series of discontinuous fields. History is this disconnected range of discursive practices. Each practice is a set of rules and procedures governing writing and thinking in a particular field. These rules govern by exclusion and regulation. Taken together the fields form a culture's 'archive', its 'positive Unconscious'.

Although the policing of knowledge is often associated with individual names (Aristotle, Plato, Aquinas, Locke, and so on), the set of structural rules which inform the various fields of knowledge is quite beyond any individual consciousness. The regulation of specific disciplines involves very refined rules for running institutions, training initiates, and transmitting knowledge. The Will-to-Knowledge exhibited in this regulation is an impersonal force. We can never know our own era's archive because it is the Unconscious from which we speak. We can understand an earlier archive only because we are utterly different and remote from it. For example, when we read the literature of the Renaissance, we often notice the richness and exuberance of its verbal play. In *The Order of Things* Foucault shows that in this period *resemblance* played a central role in the structure of all knowledges. Everything echoed everything else; nothing stood on its own. We see this vividly in the poetry of John Donne, whose mind never rests on an object but moves back and forth from spiritual to physical, human to divine, and universal to individual. In his *Devotions* he describes in cosmic terms the symptoms of the fever that almost killed him, linking the microcosm (man) and the macrocosm (universe): his tremblings are 'earthquakes', his faintings are 'eclipses', and his feverish breath 'blazing stars'. From our modern standpoint we can see the various kinds of correspondence which shape Renaissance discourses, but the writers themselves saw and thought *through* them and therefore could not see them as we see them.

Following Nietzsche Foucault denies that we can ever possess an objective knowledge of history. Historical writing will always become entangled in tropes; it can never be a science. Jeffrey Mehlman's *Revolution and Repetition* (1979) shows how Marx's *Eighteenth Brumaire* presents the 'revolution' of Louis Napoleon as a 'farcical repetition' of his uncle's revolution. Marx's historical account, according to Mehlman, acknowledges the impossibility of knowledge; there is only the absurd trope of 'repetition'. However, Foucault does not treat the strategies writers use to make sense of history as merely textual play. Such discourses are produced within a real world of power struggle. In politics, art, and science, power is gained through discourse: discourse is 'a violence that we do to things'. Claims to objectivity made on behalf of specific discourses are always spurious: there are no absolutely 'true' discourses, only more or less powerful ones.

Foucault's most distinguished American disciple is Edward Said. As a Palestinian he is attracted to Foucault's Nietzschean version of post-structuralism because it allows him to link the theory of discourse with real social and political struggles. His book on Orientalism shows how the Western image of the Orient, constructed by generations of scholars, produces myths about the laziness, deceit, and irrationality of orientals. By challenging this Western discourse Said follows the logic of Foucault's theories: no discourse is fixed for all time; it is both a cause and an effect. It not only wields power but also stimulates opposition.

In the title essay of *The World, the Text, and the Critic* (1983) Said explores the 'worldliness' of texts. He rejects the view that speech is in the world, and that texts are removed from the world, possessing only a nebulous existence in the minds of critics. He believes that recent criticism overstates the 'limitlessness' of interpretation because it cuts the connections between text and actuality. The case of Oscar Wilde suggests to Said that all attempts to divorce text from actuality are doomed to failure. Wilde tried to create an ideal world of style in which he would sum up all existence in an epigram. However, writing finally brought him into conflict with the 'normal' world. An incriminating letter signed by Wilde became a key document in the Crown's case against him. Texts are profoundly 'worldy': their use and effects are bound up with 'ownership, authority, power, and the imposition of force'.

What of the power of the critic? Said argues that when we write a critical essay, we may enter one or more of several relations with text and audience. The essay may stand *between* literary text and reader, or on the side of one of them. Said puts an interesting question concerning the real historical context of the essay: 'What is the quality of the essay's speech, toward, away from, into the *actuality*, the arena of nontextual historical vitality and presence that is taking place simultaneously with the essay itself?' The expression here is tortuous (we might say simply 'How does the essay relate to its context?'), because post-structuralist thought excludes the 'nontextual'. His words (actuality, nontextual, presence) are an affront to post-structuralism. He goes on to direct this question of context towards the more familiar Foucauldian theory: the critic can never passively transcribe the monolithic meaning of a past text, but must always write within the 'archive' of the present. Said, for example, can only speak of Wilde in terms which are sanctioned now by a prevailing discourse, which in turn is produced impersonally from the archive of the present. He claims no authority for what he says, but nevertheless tries to produce *powerful* discourse.

Structuralist critics set out to master the text and to open its secrets. Post-structuralists believe that this desire is vain because there are unconscious, or linguistic, or historical forces which cannot be mastered. The signifier floats away from the signified, *jouissance* dissolves meaning, the semiotic disrupts the symbolic, *différance* inserts a gap between signifier and signified, and power disorganises established knowledge. Post-structuralists ask questions rather than give answers; they seize upon the differences between what the text says and what it thinks it says. They set the text to work against itself, and refuse to force it to *mean* something. They deny the separateness of 'literature', and deconstruct nonliterary discourses by reading them as literature. We may be irritated by the post-structuralists' failure to arrive at conclusions, but they are only being consistent in their attempts to avoid logocentrism. However, as they often admit, their desire to resist assertions is itself doomed to failure because only by saying nothing could they prevent us from thinking that they mean something. This summary of their views itself implies their failure.

Selected Reading

Basic Texts

Barthes, Roland, *The Pleasure of the Text*, trans. R. Miller (Hill & Wang, New York, 1975).

Barthes, Roland, *S/Z*, trans. R. Miller (Hill & Wang, New York; Jonathan Cape, London, 1975).

Barthes, Roland, 'The death of the author', in *Image-Music-Text*, trans. S. Heath (Hill & Wang, New York; Fontana, London, 1977).

Bloom, Harold, *The Anxiety of Influence: A Theory of Poetry* (Oxford University Press, New York and London, 1973).

Bloom, Harold, *A Map of Misreading* (Oxford University Press, New York, Toronto, Melbourne, 1975).

Deleuze, Gilles and Guattari, Felix, *Anti-Oedipus: Capitalism and Schizophrenia* (Viking Press, New York, 1977).

de Man, Paul, *Blindness and Insight: Essays in the Rhetoric of Contemporary Criticism* (Oxford University Press, New York, 1971).

de Man, Paul, *Allegories of Reading: Figural Language in Rousseau, Nietzsche, Rilke, and Proust* (Yale University Press, New Haven, 1979).

Derrida, Jacques, *Of Grammatology*, trans. G.C. Spivak (Johns Hopkins University Press, Baltimore, 1976). The translator's preface is useful.

Derrida, Jacques, 'Signature Event Context', *Glyph*, 1 (1977), 172–97.

Foucault, Michel, *Language, Counter-Memory, Practice, Selected Essays and Interviews*, ed D.F. Bouchard (Blackwell, Oxford; Cornell University Press, Ithaca, 1977).

Harari, Josue V. (ed.), *Textual Strategies: Perspectives in Post-Structuralist Criticism* (Cornell University Press, Ithaca, 1979).

Hartman, Geoffrey H., *Criticism in the Wilderness* (Johns Hopkins University Press, Baltimore, 1980).

Johnson, Barbara, *The Critical Difference: Essays in the Contemporary Rhetoric of Reading* (Johns Hopkins University Press, Baltimore and London, 1980).

Lacan, Jacques, *Ecrits: A Selection*, trans. A. Sheridan (Tavistock, London, 1977).

Laplanche, Jean, and Pontalis, Jean-Baptiste, *The Language of Psycho-Analysis*, trans. D. Nicholson-Smith (Hogarth Press, London, 1973).

Miller, J. Hillis, 'The fiction of realism', in *Charles Dickens and George Cruickshank* (Wm Andrew Clark Memorial Library, California University Press, Los Angeles, 1971).

Ryan, Michael, *Marxism and Deconstruction: A Critical Articulation* (Johns Hopkins University Press, Baltimore and London, 1982).

Said, Edward W., *Beginnings: Intention and Method*

(Johns Hopkins University Press, Baltimore and London, 1975).

Said, Edward W., *The World, the Text, and the Critic* (Harvard University Press, Cambridge, Mass., 1983).

Searle, John, 'Reiterating the differences', *Glyph* 1 (1977), 198–208. Reply to Derrida's *Glyph* essay (above).

White, Hayden, *Tropics of Discourse* (Johns Hopkins University Press, Baltimore and London, 1978). On the use of 'tropes' in the writing of history.

Young, Robert (ed.), *Untying the Text: a Post-Structuralist Reader* (Routledge & Kegan Paul, Boston, London and Henley, 1981).

Introductions

Culler, Jonathan, 'Jacques Derrida', in *Structuralism and Since: from Lévi-Strauss to Derrida*, ed J. Sturrock (Oxford University Press, Oxford, 1979), pp. 150–80.

Jefferson, Ann, 'Structuralism and post-structuralism', in *Modern Literary Theory: a Comparative Introduction*, ed. A. Jefferson and D. Robey (Batsford, London, 1982), pp. 104–11.

Leitch, Vincent B., *Deconstructive Criticism: An Advanced Introduction* (Hutchinson, London, Melbourne, 1983).

Norris, Christopher, *Deconstruction: Theory and Practice* (Methuen, London, 1982).

Wright, Elizabeth, *Psychoanalytic Criticism: Theory in Practice* (Methuen, London and New York, 1984).

Further Reading

Atkins, G. Douglas, *Reading Deconstruction: Deconstructive Reading* (University Press of Kentucky, Lexington, 1983).

Coward, Rosalind, and Ellis, John, *Language and Materialism: Developments in Semiology and the Theory of the Subject* (Routledge &

Kegan Paul, London, 1977).

Culler, Jonathan, *On Deconstruction: Theory and Criticism after Structuralism* (Routledge & Kegan Paul, London Melbourne and Henley, 1983).

Hartman, Geoffrey H., *Saving the Text: Literature/Derrida/Philosophy* (Johns Hopkins University Press, Baltimore and London, 1981).

Lentricchia, Frank, *After the New Criticism* (Athlone Press, London, 1980). Favours Foucault and Said.

MacCabe, Colin, *The Talking Cure: Essays in Psychoanalysis and Language* (Macmillan, London and Basingstoke, 1981).

Macksey, Richard, and Donato, Eugenio (eds), *The Structuralist Controversy: The Language of Criticism and the Sciences of Man* (Johns Hopkins University Press, Baltimore and London, 1972).

Norris, Christopher, *The Deconstructive Turn: Essays in the Rhetoric of Philosophy* (Methuen, London and New York, 1983).

Wilden, Anthony, *The Language of the Self* (Johns Hopkins University Press, Baltimore, 1968). Good account of Lacan.

CHAPTER FIVE

READER-ORIENTED THEORIES

The subjective perspective

The twentieth century has seen a steady assault upon the objective certainties of nineteenth-century science. Einstein's theory of relativity alone cast doubt on the belief that objective knowledge was simply a relentless and progressive accumulation of facts. The philosopher, T.S. Kuhn, has shown that what emerges as a 'fact' in science depends upon the frame of reference which the scientific observer brings to the object of understanding. Gestalt psychology argues that the human mind does not perceive things in the world as unrelated bits and pieces but as *configurations* of elements, themes, or meaningful, organised wholes. Individual items look different in different contexts, and even within a single field of vision they will be interpreted according to whether they are seen as 'figure' or 'ground'. These approaches and others have insisted that the perceiver is active and not passive in the act of perception. In the case of the famous duck-rabbit puzzle, only the perceiver can decide how to orient the configuration of lines. Is it a duck looking left, or a rabbit looking right?

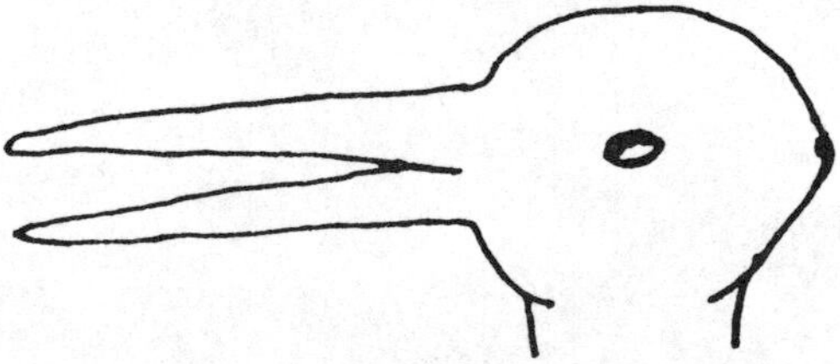

How does this modern emphasis on the observer's active role affect literary theory?

Consider Jakobson's model of linguistic communication:

CODE
ADDRESSER—MESSAGE—ADDRESSEE
CONTACT
CONTEXT

Jakobson believed that literary discourse is different from other kinds of discourse by having a 'set to the message'; a poem is about itself (its form, its imagery, its literary meaning) before it is about the poet, the reader, or the world. However, if we reject formalism and adopt the perspective of the reader or audience, the whole orientation of Jakobson's diagram changes. From this angle, we can say that the poem has no real existence until it is read; its meaning can only be discussed by its readers. We differ about interpretations only because our ways of reading differ. It is the reader who applies the code in which the message is written and in this way *actualises* what would otherwise remain only potentially meaningful. If we consider the simplest examples of interpretation, we see that the addressee is often actively involved in constructing a meaning. For example, consider the system used to represent numerals in electronic displays. The basic configuration consists of seven segments:  One might regard this figure as an imperfect square () surmounted by three sides of a similar square (), or as the reverse. The viewer's eye is invited to interpret this shape as an item in the familiar numerical system, and has no difficulty in 'recognising' an 'eight'. The viewer is able to construct the numerals without difficulty from variations of this basic configuration of segments, even though the forms offered are sometimes poor approximations:  is 2,  is 5 (not 'S'), and  is 4 (not a defective 'H'). The success of this piece of communication depends on (i) the viewer's knowledge of the number system and (ii) the viewer's ability to complete what is incomplete, or select what is significant and ignore what is not. Seen in this way the addressee is not a passive recipient of an entirely formulated meaning, but an active agent in the making of meaning. However, in this case, the addressee's task is very simply performed, because the message is stated within a completely closed system.

Consider the following poem by Wordsworth:

> A slumber did my spirit seal; } a
> I had no human fears;
> She seemed a thing that could not feel } b
> The touch of earthly years. } c
>
> } d
>
> No motion has she now, no force;
> She neither hears nor sees;
> Rolled round in earth's diurnal course,
> With rocks, and stones, and trees.

Leaving aside many preliminary and often unconscious steps which readers must make to recognise that they are reading a lyric poem, and that they accept the speaker as the authentic voice of the poet and not as a dramatic persona, we can say that there are two 'statements' made, one in each stanza: (i) I thought she could not die; (ii) She is dead. As readers we ask ourselves what sense we make of the *relationship* between the statements. Our interpretation of every phrase will turn on the answer to this question. How are we to regard the speaker's attitude towards his earlier thoughts about the female (baby, girl, or woman)? Is it good and sensible to have 'no human fears', or is it naive and foolish? Is the 'slumber' which sealed his spirit a sleep of illusion or an inspired reverie? Does 'she seemed' suggest that she had all the visible marks of an immortal being, or that the speaker was perhaps mistaken? Does the second stanza suggest that she has no spiritual existence in death and is reduced to mere inanimate matter? The first two lines of the stanza invite this view. However, the last two lines open another possible interpretation—that she has become part of a natural world and partakes of an existence which is in some sense grander than the naive spirituality of stanza one; her individual 'motion' and 'force' is now subsumed in the grand motion and force of Nature.

From the perspective of reader-oriented criticism the answers to these questions cannot simply be derived from the text. The meaning of the text is never self-formulated; the reader must act upon the textual material in order to produce meaning. Wolfgang Iser argues that literary texts always contain 'blanks' which only the reader can fill. The 'blank' between the two stanzas of Wordsworth's poem arises because the relationship between the stanzas is unstated. The act of interpretation requires us to fill this blank. A problem for theory centres on the question of whether or not the text itself triggers the reader's act of interpretation, or whether the reader's own interpretative strategies impose solutions upon the problems thrown up by the text. Even before the recent growth of reader-response theory, semioticians had developed the field with some sophistication. Umberto Eco's *The Role of the Reader* (1979; essays dating from 1959) argues that some texts are 'open' (*Finnegans Wake*, atonal music) and invite the readers' collaboration in the production of meaning, while others are 'closed' (comics, detective fiction) and predetermine the reader's response. He also speculates on how the codes available to the reader determine what the text means as it is read.

Before we survey the various ways in which the reader's role in constructing meaning has been theorised, we must deal with the question—who is 'the reader'?

Gerald Prince: the 'narratee'

Gerald Prince asks the question—why, when we study novels, do we take such pains to discriminate between the various kinds of narrator (omniscient, unreliable, implied author, etc.), but never ask questions about the different kinds of person to whom the narrator addresses the discourse. Prince calls this person the 'narratee'. We must not confuse the narratee with the reader. The narrator may specify a narratee in terms of sex ('Dear Madam...'), class ('gentlemen'), situation (the 'reader' in his armchair), race (white), or age (mature). Evidently actual readers may or may not coincide with the person addressed by the narrator. An actual reader may be a black, male, young miner reading in bed. The narratee is also distinguished from the 'virtual reader' (the sort of reader whom the author has in mind when developing the narrative) and the 'ideal reader' (the perfectly insightful reader who understands the writer's every move).

How do we learn to identify narratees? When Trollope writes 'Our archdeacon was worldly—who among us is not so?', we understand that the narratees here are people who, like the narrator, recognise the fallibility of all human beings, even the most pious. There are many 'signals', direct and indirect, which contribute to our knowledge of the narratee. The assumptions of the narratee may be attacked, supported, queried, or solicited by the narrator who will thereby strongly imply the narratee's character. When the narrator apologises for certain inadequacies in the discourse ('I cannot convey this experience in words'), this indirectly tell us something of the narratee's susceptibilities and values. Even in a novel which appears to make no direct reference to a narratee we pick up tiny signals even in the simplest of literary figures. The second term of a comparison, for example, often indicates the kind of world familiar to the narratee ('the song was as sincere as a TV jingle'). Sometimes the narratee is an important character. For example, in *A Thousand and One Nights* the very survival of the narrator, Scheherazade, depends on the continued attention of the narratee, the caliph; if he loses interest in her stories, she must die. The effect of Prince's elaborated theory is to highlight a dimension of narration which had been understood intuitively by readers but which had remained shadowy and undefined. He contributes to reader-oriented theory by drawing attention to ways in which narratives produce their own 'readers' or 'listeners', who may or may not coincide with actual readers. Many of the writers discussed in the following pages ignore this distinction between reader and narratee.

Phenomenology

A modern philosophical tendency which stresses the perceiver's central role in determining meaning is known as 'phenomenology'. According to Husserl the proper object of philosophical investigation is the contents of our consciousness and not objects in the world. Consciousness is always of something, and it is the 'something' which appears to our consciousness which is truly real to us. In addition, argued Husserl, we discover in the things which appear in consciousness ('phenomena' in Greek, meaning 'things appearing') their universal or essential qualities. Phenomenology claims to show us the underlying nature both of human consciousness and of 'phenomena'. This was an attempt to revive the idea (eclipsed since the Romantics) that the individual human mind is the centre and origin of all meaning. In literary theory this approach did not encourage a purely subjective concern for the critic's mental structure but a type of criticism which tries to enter into the world of a writer's works and to arrive at an understanding of the underlying nature or essence of the writings as they appear to the critic's consciousness. The early work of J. Hillis Miller, the American critic, was influenced by the phenomenological theories of the so-called Geneva School of critics, who included Georges Poulet and Jean Starobinski. Miller's study of Thomas Hardy, for example, uncovers the novels' pervasive mental structures, namely 'distance' and 'desire'. The act of interpretation is possible, because the texts allow the reader access to the author's consciousness, which, says Poulet, 'is open to me, welcomes me, lets me look deep inside itself, and . . . allows me . . . to think what it thinks and feel what it feels'. Derrida (see chapter 4) would consider this kind of thinking 'logocentric' for supposing that a meaning is centred on a 'transcendental subject' (the author) and can be recentred on another such subject (the reader).

The shift towards a reader-oriented theory is prefigured in the rejection of Husserl's 'objective' view by his pupil Martin Heidegger. The latter argued that what is distinctive about human existence is its *Dasein* ('givenness'): our consciousness both *projects* the things of the world and at the same time *is subjected* to the world by the very nature of existence in the world. We find ourselves 'flung down' into the world, into a time and place we did not choose, but at the same time it is our world in so far as our consciousness projects it. We can never adopt an attitude of detached contemplation, looking down upon the world as if from a mountain top. We are inevitably merged with the very object of our consciousness. Our thinking is always in a situation and is therefore always *historical*, although this history is not external and social but personal and inward. It was Hans-Georg Gadamer who in *Truth and Method* (1975) applied Heidegger's situational approach to literary theory. Gadamer argued that a literary work does not pop into the world as a finished and neatly parcelled bundle of meaning. Meaning depends on the historical situation of the interpreter. Gadamer influenced 'reception theory' (see Jauss below).

Wolfgang Iser: the 'implied reader'

In Iser's view the critic's task is not to explain the text as an object but rather its effects on the reader. It is in the nature of texts to allow a spectrum of possible readings. The term 'reader' can be subdivided into 'implied reader' and 'actual reader'. The first is the reader whom the text creates for itself and amounts to 'a network of response-inviting structures', which predispose us to read in certain ways. The 'actual reader' receives certain mental images in the process of reading; however, the images will inevitably be coloured by the reader's 'existing stock of experience'. If we are atheists we will be affected differently by Wordsworth's poem than if we are Christians. The experience of reading will differ according to our past experiences.

The words we read do not represent actual objects but human speech in fictional guise. This fictional language helps us to construct in our minds *imaginary* objects. To take Iser's example, in *Tom Jones* Fielding presents two characters, Allworthy (the perfect man) and Captain Blifil (the hypocrite). The reader's imaginary object, 'the perfect man', is subject to modification: when Allworthy is taken in by Blifil's feigned piety, we adjust the imaginary object in view of the perfect man's lack of judgement. The reader's journey through the book is a continuous process of such adjustments. We hold in our minds certain expectations, based on our memory of characters and events, but the expectations are continually modified, and the memories transformed as we pass through the text. What we grasp as we read is only a series of changing viewpoints, not something fixed and fully meaningful at every point.

While a literary work does not represent objects, it does refer to the extra-literary world by selecting certain norms, value systems or 'world-views'. These norms are concepts of reality which help human beings to make sense of the chaos of their experience. The text adopts a 'repertoire' of such norms and suspends their validity within its fictional world. In *Tom Jones*, various characters embody different norms: Allworthy (benevolence), Squire Western (ruling passion), Square (the eternal fitness of things), Thwackum (the human mind as a sink of iniquity), Sophia (the ideality of natural inclinations). Each norm asserts certain values at the expense of others, and each tends to contract the image of human nature to a single principle or perspective. The reader is therefore impelled by the unfinished nature of the text to relate the values of the hero (good nature) to the various norms which are violated by the hero in specific incidents. *Only the reader* can actualise the degree to which particular norms are to be rejected or questioned. *Only the reader* can make the complex moral judgement on Tom, and see that, while his 'good nature' disrupts the restrictive norms of other characters, it does so partly because Tom lacks 'prudence' and 'circumspection'. Fielding doesn't tell us this, but as readers we insert this into the interpretation in order to fill a 'gap' in the text. In real life we sometimes meet people who appear to represent certain world-views ('cynicism', 'humanism'), but we assign such descriptions ourselves on the basis of received ideas. The value systems we encounter are met at random: no author selects and predetermines them and no hero appears in order to test their validity. So, even though there are 'gaps' in the text to be filled, the text is much more definitely structured than life.

If we apply Iser's method to our Wordsworth poem, we see that the reader's activity consists in first adjusting his or her viewpoint ((a), (b), (c), then (d)), and secondly in filling a 'blank' between the two stanzas (between transcendent spirituality and pantheistic immanence). This application may seem rather unwieldy because a short poem doesn't require the reader to make the long sequence of adjustments necessary when reading a novel. However, the concept of 'gaps' remains valid.

It remains unclear whether Iser wishes to grant the reader the power to fill up at will the blanks in the text or whether he regards the text as the final arbiter of the reader's actualisations. Is the gap between 'the perfect man' and 'the perfect man's lack of judgement' filled by a freely judging reader or by a reader who is *guided* by the text's instructions? Iser's emphasis is ultimately phenomenological: the reader's experience of reading is at the centre of the literary process. By resolving the contradictions between the various viewpoints which emerge from the text or by filling the 'gaps' between viewpoints in various ways, the readers take the text into their consciousnesses and make it their own *experience*. It seems that, while texts do set the terms on which the reader actualises meanings, the reader's own 'store of experience' will take some part in the process. The reader's existing consciousness will have to make certain internal adjustments in order to receive and process the alien viewpoints which the text presents as reading takes place. This situation produces the possibility that the reader's own 'world-view' may be modified as a result of internalising, negotiating and realising the partially indeterminate elements of the text. We may learn something from reading! To use Iser's words, reading 'gives us the chance to formulate the unformulated'.

Hans Robert Jauss: horizons of expectations

Jauss, an important German exponent of 'reception' theory (*Rezeption-ästhetik*), has given a historical dimension to reader-oriented criticism. He tries to achieve a compromise between Russian Formalism which ignores history, and social theories which ignore the text. Writing during a period of social unrest at the end of the 1960s, Jauss and others wanted to question the old canon of German literature *and* to show that it was perfectly reasonable to do so. The older critical outlook had ceased to make sense in the same way that Newton's physics no longer seemed adequate in the early twentieth-century. He borrows from the philosophy of science (T.S. Kuhn) the term 'paradigm' which refers to the scientific framework of concepts and assumptions operating in a particular period. 'Ordinary science' does its experimental work within the mental world of a particular paradigm, until a new paradigm displaces the old one and throws up new problems and establishes new assumptions. Jauss uses the term 'horizon and expectations' to describe the criteria readers use to judge literary texts in any given period. These criteria will help the reader decide how to judge a poem as for example an epic, or a tragedy or a pastoral; it will also, in a more general way, cover what is to be regarded as poetic or literary as opposed to unpoetic or non-literary uses of languages. Ordinary writing and reading will work within such a horizon. For example, if we consider the English Augustan period, we might say that Pope's poetry was judged according to criteria which were based upon values of clarity, naturalness, and stylistic decorum (the words should be adjusted according to the dignity of the subject). However, this does not establish once and for all the value of Pope's poetry. During the second half of the eighteenth century commentators began to question whether Pope was a poet at all and to suggest that he was a clever versifier who put prose into rhyming couplets, and lacked the imaginative power required of true poetry. Omitting the next century, we can say that modern readings of Pope work within a changed horizon of expectations: we now often value his poems for their wit, complexity, moral insight, and their renewal of literary tradition.

The original horizon of expectations only tells us how the work was valued and interpreted when it appeared, but does not establish its meaning finally. In Jauss's view it would be equally wrong to say that a work is universal, that its meaning is fixed forever and open to all readers in any period: 'A literary work is not an object which stands by itself and which offers the same face to each reader in each period. It is not a monument which reveals its timeless essence in a monologue'. This means, of course, that we will never be able to survey the successive horizons which flow from the time of a work down to the present day and then, with an Olympian detachment, to sum up the work's final value or meaning. To do so would be to ignore our own historical situation. Whose authority are we to accept? That of the first readers? The combined opinion of readers over time? Or the aesthetic judgement of the present? The first readers may have been incapable of seeing the revolutionary significance of a writer (this applies, for example, to William Blake). The same objection must also apply to succeeding readers' judgements, including our own.

Jauss's answers to these questions derive from the philosophical 'hermeneutics' of Hans-Georg Gadamer, a follower of Heidegger (see p. 111). Gadamer argues that all interpretations of past literature arise from a dialogue between past and present. Our attempts to understand a work will depend on the questions which our own cultural environment allows us to raise. At the same time, we seek to discover the questions which the work itself was trying to answer in its own dialogue with history. Our present perspective always involves a relationship to the past, but at the same time the past can only be grasped through the limited perspective of the present. Put in this way, the task of establishing a *knowledge* of the past seems hopeless. But a hermeneutical notion of 'understanding' does not separate knower and object in the familiar fashion of empirical science, but views understanding as a 'fusion' of past and present: we cannot make our journey into the past without taking the present with us. 'Hermeneutics' was a term originally applied to the interpretation of sacred texts; its modern equivalent preserves the same serious and reverent attitude towards the texts to which it tries to gain access.

Jauss recognises that a writer may directly affront the prevailing expectations of his or her day. Indeed, reception theory itself developed in Germany during the 1960s in a climate of literary change: writers such as Rolf Hochhuth, Hans Magnus Enzensberger and Peter Handke were challenging accepted literary formalism by increasing the direct involvement of reader or audience. Jauss himself examines the case of Baudelaire whose *Les fleurs du mal* created uproar and attracted legal prosecution. It offended the norms of bourgeois morality *and* the canons of romantic poetry. However, the poems also immediately produced a new aesthetic horizon of expectations; the literary avant-garde saw the book as a trail-blazing work of decadence. In the later nineteenth century the poems were 'concretised' as expressions of the aesthetic cult of nihilism. Jauss assesses later psychological, linguistic, and sociological interpretations of Baudelaire's poems, but often disregards them. One is left unhappy about a method which recognises its own historical limitations but still feels able to regard certain other interpretations as raising 'falsely posed or illegitimate questions'. The 'fusion of horizons' is not, it seems, a total merging of all the points of view which have arisen but only those which to the hermeneutical sense of the critic appear to be part of the gradually emerging totality of meanings which make up the true unity of the text.

Stanley Fish: the reader's experience

Stanley Fish, the American critic of seventeenth-century English Literaure, has developed a reader-oriented perspective called an 'affective stylistics'. Like Iser he concentrates on the adjustments of expectation to be made by readers as they pass along the text, but considers this at the immediately local level of the sentence. He separates his approach very self-consciously from all kinds of formalism (including American New Criticism) by denying literary language any special status; we use the same reading strategies to interpret literary and non-literary sentences. His attention is directed to the developing responses of the reader in relation to the words of sentences as they succeed one another in time. Describing the fallen angels' state of awareness, having plummeted from heaven to hell, Milton wrote 'Nor did they not perceive the evil plight'. This cannot be treated as a statement equivalent to 'they perceived the evil plight'. We must attend, argues Fish, to the sequence of words which creates a state of suspension in the reader, who hangs between two views of the fallen angels' awareness. His point is weakened though not refuted by the fact that Milton was evidently imitating the double negative in the style of classical epic. The following sentence by Walter Pater receives an especially sensitive analysis by Fish; 'This at least of flame-like, our life has, that it is but the concurrence, renewed from moment to moment, of forces parting sooner or later on their ways'. He points out that by interrupting 'concurrence of forces' with 'renewed from moment to moment' Pater prevents the reader from establishing a definite or stable image in the mind, and at each stage in the sentence forces the reader to make an adjustment in expectation and interpretation. The idea of 'the concurrence' is disrupted by 'parting', but then 'sooner or later' leaves the 'parting' temporally uncertain. The reader's expectation of meaning is thus continuously adjusted: the meaning is the total movement of reading.

Jonathan Culler has lent general support to Fish's aims, but has criticised him for failing to give us a proper theoretical formulation of his reader criticism. Fish believes that his readings of sentences simply follow the natural practice of informed readers. In his view a reader is someone who possesses a 'linguistic competence'; such a reader has internalised the

to fall straight downward

distressing situation

syntactic and semantic knowledge required for reading. The 'informed reader' of literary texts has also acquired a specifically 'literary competence' (knowledge of literary conventions). Culler makes two trenchant criticisms of Fish's position. (i) He fails to theorise the conventions of reading; that is, he fails to ask the question 'What conventions do readers follow when they read?' (ii) His claim to read sentences word by word in a temporal sequence is misleading: there is no reason to believe that readers actually do take in sentences in such a piecemeal and gradual way. Why does he assume, for example, that the reader, faced with Milton's 'Nor did they not perceive', will experience a sense of being suspended between two views? There is something factitious about Fish's continual willingness to be surprised by the next word in a sequence. Also, Fish himself admits that his approach tends to privilege those texts which proceed in a self-undermining way (*Self-Consuming Artifacts* is the title of one of his books).

In *Is There a Text in This Class?* (1980) Fish acknowledges that his earlier books treated his own experience of reading as the norm, and goes on to justify his earlier position by introducing the idea of 'interpretive communities'. This means that Fish was trying to persuade readers to adopt 'a set of community assumptions so that when they read they would do what I did'. Of course, there may be many different groups of readers who adopt particular kinds of reading strategies (e.g. Fishian strategies!). In this latest phase of his work the strategies of a particular interpretive community determine the entire process of reading — the stylistic facts of the texts and the experience of reading them. If we accept the category of interpretive communities, we no longer need to choose between asking questions about the text or about the reader; the whole problem of subject and object disappears.

Michael Riffaterre: literary competence

Michael Riffaterre agrees with the Russian Formalists in regarding poetry as a special use of language. Ordinary language is practical and is used to refer to some sort of 'reality', while poetic language focuses on the message as an end in itself.

He takes this formalist view from Jakobson, but in a well-known essay he attacks Jakobson's and Lévi-Strauss' interpretation of Baudelaire's 'Les Chats'. Riffaterre shows that the linguistic features they discover in the poem could not possibly be perceived even by an informed reader. All manner of grammatical and phonemic patterns are thrown up by their structuralist approach, but not all the features they note can be part of the poetic structure for the reader. In a telling example he objects to their claim that by concluding a line with the word *volupté* (rather than, say, *plaisir*) Baudelaire is making play with the fact that a feminine noun (*la volupté*) is used as a 'masculine' rhyme, thus creating sexual ambiguity in the poem. Riffaterre rightly points out that a reasonably practised reader may well never have heard of the technical terms 'masculine' and 'feminine' rhyme! However, Riffaterre has some difficulty in explaining why something perceived by Jakobson does not count as evidence of what readers perceive in a text. What do you have to do to get your reader's licence?

Riffaterre developed his theory in *Semiotics of Poetry* (1978), in which he argues that competent readers go beyond surface meaning. If we regard a poem as a string of statements, we are limiting our attention to its 'meaning', which is merely what it can be said to represent in units of information. If we attend only to a poem's 'meaning' we reduce it to a (possibly nonsensical) string of unrelated bits. A true response starts by noticing that the elements (signs) in a poem often appear to depart from normal grammar or normal representation: the poem seems to be establishing significance only *indirectly* and in doing so 'threatens the literary representation of reality'. It requires only ordinary linguistic competence to understand the poem's 'meaning', but the reader requires 'literary competence' to deal with the frequent 'ungrammaticalities' encountered in reading a poem. Faced with the stumbling block of ungrammaticalness the reader is forced, during the process of reading, to uncover a second (higher) level of significance which will explain the ungrammatical features of the text. What will ultimately be uncovered is a structural 'matrix', which can be reduced to a single sentence or even a single word. The matrix can be deduced only indirectly and is not actually present as a word or statement in the poem. The poem is connected to its matrix by actual versions of the matrix in the form of familiar statements, clichés, quotations, or conventional associations. These versions are called 'hypograms'. It is the matrix which ultimately gives a poem unity. This reading process can be summarised as follows:

(i) Try to read for ordinary 'meaning'.
(ii) Highlight those elements which appear ungrammatical and which obstruct an ordinary mimetic interpretation.
(iii) Discover the 'hypograms' (or commonplaces) which receive expanded or unfamiliar expression in the text.
(iv) Derive the 'matrix' from the 'hypograms'; that is, find a single statement or word capable of generating the 'hypograms' and the text.

If we tried, hesitantly, to apply this theory to the Wordsworth poem 'A slumber did my spirit seal' (see p. 108), we might finally arrive at the matrix 'spirit and matter'. The 'hypograms' which are reworked in the text appear to be (i) death is the end of life; (ii) the human spirit cannot die; (iii) in death we return to the earth from which we came. The poem achieves unity by reworking these commonplaces in an unexpected way from a basic matrix. No doubt Riffaterre's theory would have looked stronger if I had given one of his own examples from Baudelaire or Gautier. His approach seems much more appropriate as a way of reading difficult poetry which goes against the grain of 'normal' grammar or semantics. As a general theory of reading it has many difficulties, not least that it disallows several kinds of reading that you or I might think perfectly straightforward (for example reading a poem for its political message).

Jonathan Culler: conventions of reading

Jonathan Culler has argued that a theory of reading has to uncover the interpretative operations used by readers. We all know that different readers produce different interpretations. While this has led some theorists to despair of developing a theory of reading at all, Culler argues that it is this variety of interpretation which theory has to explain. While readers may differ about meaning, they may well follow the same set of interpretative conventions. His first example is New Criticism's basic assumption—that of unity; different readers may discover unity in different ways in a particular text, but the basic forms of meaning they look for (forms of unity) may be the same. While we may feel no compulsion to perceive the unity of our experiences in the real world, in the case of poems we often expect to find it. Returning to the Wordsworth poem, discussed above, a reader will find it very difficult not to ask the question 'How can I unify the two halves of the poem?' However, the variety of interpretations arises because there are several models of unity which one may bring to bear, and within a particular model there are several ways of applying it to the poem. One model is thematic unity. The Wordsworth poem may be unified as 'pantheistic' or 'nihilistic'. Alternatively we may discover unity by using a model of '*alethic reversal*: first a false or inadequate vision, then its true or adequate counterpart' (Culler). If we apply this to the Wordsworth poem, we might see a transition from an inadequate vision of the superiority of otherworldy spirituality to a more adequate vision of union with nature. It can certainly be claimed for Culler's approach that it allows a genuine prospect of a theoretical advance, unlike Fish's which gives us a useful method but shuts its eyes to the fundamental issues of theory, or Riffaterre's which produces a theoretical strait-jacket. On the other hand, one can object to Culler's refusal to examine the *content* of particular interpretative moves. For example, he examines two political readings of Blake's 'London' and concludes: 'The accounts different readers offer of what is wrong with the social system will, of course, differ, but the formal interpretative operations that give them a structure to fill in seem very similar'. There is something narrow about a theory which treats interpretative moves as substantial and the content of the moves as immaterial. After all, there may be historical grounds for regarding one way of applying an interpretative model as more valid or plausible than another. Readings of different degrees of plausibility may well share the same interpretative conventions. It is, for example, more plausible to regard the Wordsworth poem as 'pantheistic' than 'nihilistic' (although neither view is fully satisfactory).

As we have seen, Culler, in *Structuralist Poetics*, argued that a theory of the structure of texts or genres is not possible because there is no underlying form of 'competence' which produces them. We can talk only about the competence of readers to make sense of what they read. Poets and novelists write on the basis of this competence: they write what can be read. In order to read texts as literature we must possess a 'literary competence', just as we need a more general 'linguistic competence' to make sense of the ordinary linguistic utterances we encounter. We acquire this 'grammar' of literature in educational institutions. Culler recognised that the conventions which apply to one genre will not apply to another, and that the conventions of interpretation will differ from one period to another, but as a structuralist he believed that theory is concerned with static, synchronic systems of meaning and not diachronic historical ones.

Norman Holland and David Bleich: reader psychology

Two American critics have derived approaches to reader theory from psychology. Norman Holland adopts a specific theory, according to which every child receives the imprint of a 'primary identity' from its mother. The adult has an 'identity theme' which, like a musical theme, is capable of variation but remains a central structure of stable identity. When we read a text, we process it in accordance with our identity theme. We 'use the literary work to symbolize and finally replicate ourselves'. We recast the work to discover our own characteristic strategies for coping with the deep fears and wishes that shape our psychic lives. The reader's inbuilt defence mechanisms must be placated to allow access to the text. A dramatic example is a case cited by Holland of a boy compulsively driven to read detective stories to satisfy his aggressive feelings towards his mother by allying himself with the murderer. The stories not only took the imprint of his desires but also allowed him to assuage his guilt by associating himself with the victim and also the detective. In this way the boy was able to gratify his instincts *and* to set up defences against anxiety and guilt. The example is untypical but raises a number of questions about Holland's theory. In more typical instances, readers assert control over texts by discovering unifying themes and structures in them which enable the readers to internalise the text—'Putting within yourself and so controlling something that is outside where it cannot be controlled but seeks to control you'. Holland emphasises the interplay between the reader's identity theme and the text's unity: the latter is discovered by the reader as an expression of his or her identity theme. However, the example of the boy seems to invalidate the notions of textual 'unity' and 'identity theme'. *Any* detective story allowed him to construct the meanings he needed psychically; if there was a textual unity it seemed to lie in the narrative structure of detective stories rather than in specific texts. In any case the boy's reading seems to have *disrupted* the texts' unity by producing contradictory subject positions for him to enter. Indeed this example (admittedly not pursued by Holland) throws into doubt the whole notion of an identity theme as a principle of psychic *unity*. Our discussion of Lacan suggested one alternate model (Chapter 4).

David Bleich's *Subjective Criticism* (1978) is a sophisticated argument in favour of a shift from an objective to a subjective paradigm in critical theory. He argues that modern philosophers of science (especially T.S. Kuhn) have correctly denied the existence of an objective world of facts. Even in science, the perceiver's mental structures will decide what counts as an objective fact: 'Knowledge is made by people and not found', because 'the object of observation appears changed by the act of observation'. He goes on to insist that the advances of 'knowledge' are determined by the *needs of the community*. When we say that 'science' has replaced 'superstition', we are describing not a passage from darkness to light, but a change in paradigm which occurs when certain urgent needs of the community come into conflict with old beliefs and demand new beliefs.

The child's acquisition of language, argues Bleich, enables it to establish a subjective control of experience. We can understand another's words only as a 'motivated act'—as a way of establishing some grasp of things which has importance for the speaker. Every utterance indicates an *intention* and every act of interpreting an utterance is a *conferring* of meaning. Since this is true of all human attempts to explain experience, we can best understand the arts if we ask—what are the motives of those who create 'symbolic' renderings of experience? What are the individual and communal occasions for their response and creativity?

'Subjective criticism' is based on the assumption that 'each person's most urgent motivations are to understand himself'. In his classroom experiments Bleich was led to distinguish between (i) the reader's spontaneous 'response' to a text, and (ii) the 'meaning' the reader attributed to it. The latter is usually presented as an 'objective' interpretation (something offered for negotiation in a pedagogic situation), but is necessarily developed from the *subjective response* of the reader. Whatever system of thought is being employed (moral, Marxist, structuralist, psychoanalytic), interpretations of particular texts will normally reflect the subjective individuality of a personal 'response'. Without a grounding in 'response', the application of systems of thought will be dismissed as empty formulae derived from received dogma. Particular interpretations make more sense when critics take the trouble to explain the growth and origin of their views. In the teaching situation this is provided by a 'response statement', which gives the 'motivational substrate' of the subsequent interpretative judgement. For example, Ms A's 'response' to Kafka's 'Metamorphosis' was one of initial repulsion, 'like taking cod-liver oil'. Ms A felt sadness at the plight of Gregor because she identified him with her brother who was similarly humiliated by and alienated from his father. The transformation of Gregor to a dung beetle produced a conflicting repulsion, since Ms A confessed to her sadistic insensitivity to insects. There was a further association between Gregor and memories of an ugly schoolgirl about which Ms A also felt guilty. Her predominant feelings for all the characters, but especially Gregor, were ambivalent ('attraction-repulsion'). The final judgement of 'meaning' which emerges from Ms A's statement has an objective appearance but is evidently built upon the initial 'response': the story is 'structured on the drama of the victim/victimiser dualism'. Victims and victimisers, she argues, depend on one another and in the end cannot be distinguished. In other words, Ms A projects her own inconsistency of attitudes towards people into the text, and discovers there a 'dualism'. Anyone taking part in a seminar on the story would be inclined to see Ms A's interpretation as an 'objective' statement, offered in a suitably detached literary critical idiom. However, 'subjective criticism' would wish to reconnect the interpretation to Ms A's personal 'response' and its subjective motivation.

Reader-oriented theory, like feminist criticism, has no single or predominant philosophical starting point. The writers we have considered belong to quite different traditions of thought. The German writers, Iser and Jauss, draw upon phenomenology and hermeneutics in their attempts to describe the process of reading in terms of the reader's consciousness. Riffaterre presupposes a reader who possesses a specifically *literary* competence, while Stanley Fish believes that readers respond to the sequence of words in sentences whether or not the sentences are literary. Jonathan Culler tries to establish a 'structuralist' theory of interpretation which seeks to disclose the regularities in readers' strategies, while recognising that the same strategies can produce different interpretations. In Chapter 4 we saw how Roland Barthes celebrates the end of structuralism's reign by granting the reader the power to create meanings by 'opening' the text to the interminable play of 'codes'. The Americans, Holland and Bleich, regard reading as a process which satisfies or at least depends upon the psychological needs of the reader. Whatever one thinks of these reader-oriented theories, there is no doubt that they seriously challenge the predominance of the text-oriented theories of New Criticism and Formalism. We can no longer talk about the meaning of a text without considering the reader's contribution to it.

Selected Reading

Basic Texts

Bleich, David, *Subjective Criticism* (Johns Hopkins University Press, Baltimore and London, 1978).

Culler, Jonathan, *The Pursuit of Signs: Semiotics, Literature, Deconstruction* (Routledge & Kegan Paul, London and Henley,

1981), especially Part Two.

Eco, Umberto, *The Role of the Reader: Explorations in the Semiotics of Texts* (Indiana University Press, Bloomington, 1979).

Fish, Stanley, *Self-Consuming Artifacts: The Experience of Seventeenth-Century Literature* (California University Press, Berkely, 1972).

Fish, Stanley, *Is There a Text in This Class?* (Harvard University Press, Cambridge, Mass., 1980).

Holland, Norman, *5 Readers Reading* (Yale University Press, New Haven and London, 1975).

Ingarden, Roman, *The Literary Work of Art*, trans. George G. Grabowicz (Northwestern University Press, Evanston, I11., 1973).

Iser, Wolfgang, *The Act of Reading: A Theory of Aesthetic Response* (Johns Hopkins University Press, Baltimore, 1978)

Jauss, Hans R., *Toward An Aesthetic of Reception*, trans. T. Bahti (Harvester Press, Brighton, 1982). The important first chapter is also in Ralph Cohen (ed.), *New Directions in Literary History* (Routledge & Kegan Paul, London, 1974).

Prince, Gerald, 'Introduction to the study of the narratee', in Tompkins (below). French original in *Poétique* no. 14 (1973), 177–96.

Riffaterre, Michael, 'Describing poetic structures: two approaches to Baudelaire's *Les Chats*', in J. Ehrmann (ed.), *Structuralism* (Doubleday & Co., Inc., Garden City, New York, 1970). Extract in Tompkins. Originally *Yale French Studies*, 36–7 (1966), 200–42.

Riffaterre, Michael, *Semiotics of Poetry* (Indiana University Press, and Methuen, London, 1978).

Suleiman, Susan, and Crosman, Inge (eds.), *The Reader in the Text: Essays on Audience and Interpretation*. (Princeton University Press,

Princeton, N.J., 1980). Includes essays by Iser, Culler, Prince and Holland.

Tompkins, Jane P., (ed.), *Reader-Response Criticism: From Formalism to Post-Structuralism.* (Johns Hopkins University Press, Baltimore, 1980). Basic anthology of texts.

Introductions

Introductions to Suleiman and Crosman, *The Reader in the Text* (above) and Tompkins, *Reader-Response Criticism* (above).

Eagleton, Terry, *Literary Theory: An Introduction* (Blackwell, Oxford, 1983). chap. 2.

Fokkema, D.W., and Kunne-Ibsch, E., *The Theories of Literature in the Twentieth Century: Structuralism, Marxism, Aesthetics of Reception, Semiotics* (C. Hurst, London, 1977).

Holub, Robert C., *Reception Theory: A Critical Introduction* (Methuen, London and New York, 1984).

CHAPTER SIX

FEMINIST CRITICISM

Women writers and women readers have always had to work against the grain. Aristotle declared that 'the female is female by virtue of a certain lack of qualities', and St Thomas Aquinas believed that woman is an 'imperfect man'. When Donne wrote 'Air and Angels' he alluded to (but did not refute) Aquinas' theory that form is masculine and matter feminine: the superior, godlike, male intellect impresses its form upon the malleable, inert, female matter. In pre-Mendelian days men regarded their sperm as the active seeds which give form to the waiting ovum which lacks identity till it receives the male's impress. In Aeschylus' trilogy, *The Oresteia*, victory is granted by Athena to the male argument, put by Apollo, that the mother is no parent to her child. The victory of the male principle of intellect brings to an end the reign of the sensual female Furies and asserts patriarchy over matriarchy. Feminist criticism sometimes summons up the anger of the Furies in order to disturb the complacent certainties of patriarchal culture and to create a less oppressive climate for women writers and readers. Sometimes feminist critics have employed wit to 'deconstruct' male-dominated ways of seeing. Mary Ellmann, for example, suggests that we might prefer to regard the ovum as daring, independent, and individualistic (rather than 'apathetic') and the sperm as conforming and sheeplike (rather than 'enthusiastic'). Woody Allen's fantasy of a panic-stricken sperm passively awaiting the journey into the unknown is as unheroic about insemination as any feminist could wish!

Problems of feminist theory

Some feminists do not wish to embrace 'theory' at all. There are many reasons for this. In academic institutions 'theory' is often male, even macho; it is the hard, intellectual, avant-garde of literary studies. The manly virtues of rigour, thrusting purpose, and rampant ambition find their home in 'theory' rather than in the often tender art of critical interpretation. Feminists have often exposed the fraudulent objectivity of male science. Freud's theories have been castigated for their blatant sexism, for example, for their assumption that female sexuality is shaped by 'penis-envy'. Much feminist criticism wishes to escape the 'fixities and definites' of theory and to develop a female discourse which cannot be tied down conceptually as belonging to a recognised (and therefore probably male-produced) theoretical tradition. However, feminists *have* been attracted to the Lacanian and Derridean types of post-structuralist theory, perhaps because they actually refuse to assert a 'masculine' authority or truth. The psychoanalytic theories about instinctive drives have been especially helpful to feminist critics who have tried to articulate the subversive and apparently formless resistance of some women writers and critics to male-dominated literary values, although a few feminists have managed to evoke the possible strategies of female resistance without elaborate theorising.

Simone de Beauvoir, in *The Second Sex* (1949), established with great clarity the fundamental questions of modern feminism. When a woman tries to define herself, she starts by saying 'I am a woman'. No man would do so. This fact reveals the basic asymmetry between the terms 'masculine' and 'feminine'. Man defines the human, not woman. This imbalance goes back to the Old Testament. Being dispersed among men, women have no separate history, no natural solidarity; they have not combined as other oppressed groups have. Woman is riveted into a lop-sided relationship with man; he is the One, she the Other. Man's dominance has secured an ideological climate of compliance: 'Legislators, priests, philosophers, writers, and scientists have striven to show that the subordinate position of woman is willed in heaven and advantageous on earth.' De Beauvoir documents her argument with great erudition. Women have been *made* inferiors and the oppression has been compounded by men's belief that women *are* inferiors by nature. The abstract notion of 'equality' receives lip-service, but demands for real equality will usually be resisted. Women themselves, not sympathetic men, are in the best position to assess the true existential possibilities of womanhood.

There appear to be five main foci involved in most discussions of sexual difference:

biology
experience
discourse
the unconscious
social and economic conditions

Arguments which treat biology as fundamental and which play down socialisation have been used mainly by men to keep women in their 'place'. The saying '*Tota mulier in utero*' ('Woman is nothing but a womb') sums up this attitude. If a woman's body is her destiny, then all attempts to question attributed sex roles will fly in the face of the natural order. On the other hand, some radical feminists celebrate women's biological attributes as sources of superiority rather than inferiority. Any extreme argument for the special nature of women runs the risk of landing up, by a different route, in the same position occupied by male chauvinists. This risk is also run by those who appeal to the special experience of woman as the source of positive female values in life and in art. Since only women, the argument goes, have undergone those specifically female life-experiences (ovulation, menstruation, parturition), only they can speak of a woman's life. Further, a woman's experience includes a different perceptual and emotional life; women do not see things in the same ways as men, and have different ideas and feelings about what is important or not important. The study of the literary representation of these differences in women's writing has been called 'gynocritics'. The third focus, discourse, has received a great deal of attention by feminists. Dale Spender's *Man-Made Language*, as the title suggests, considers that women have been fundamentally oppressed by a male-dominated language. If we accept Foucault's argument that what is 'true' depends on who controls discourse, then it is reasonable to believe that men's domination of discourses has trapped women inside a male 'truth'. From this point of view it makes sense for women writers to contest men's control of language rather than merely to retreat into a ghetto of feminine discourse. The opposite view is taken by the sociolinguist Robin Lakoff who believes that women's language actually is inferior, since it contains patterns of 'weakness' and 'uncertainty', focuses on the 'trivial', the frivolous, the unserious, and stresses personal emotional responses. Male utterance, she argues, is 'stronger' and should be adopted by women if they wish to achieve social equality with men. Most radical feminists take the view that women have been brain-washed by this type of patriarchal ideology which produces stereotypes of strong men and feeble women. The psychoanalytic theories of Lacan and Kristeva have provided a fourth focus—the process of the unconscious. Some feminist writers have broken completely with biologism by associating the 'female' with those processes which tend to undermine the authority of 'male' discourse. Whatever encourages or initiates a free play of meanings and prevents 'closure' is regarded as 'female'. Female sexuality is revolutionary, subversive, heterogeneous, and 'open'. This approach is less likely to run the risks of ghettoisation and stereotyping, since it refuses to define female sexuality; if there is a female principle, it is simply to remain outside the male definition of the female. Virginia Woolf was the first woman critic to include a sociological dimension (fifth focus) in her analysis of women's writing. Since then, Marxist feminists, in particular, have tried to relate changing social and economic conditions and the changing balance of power between the sexes. They agree with other feminists in rejecting the notion of a universal femininity.

Kate Millett and Michèle Barrett: political feminism

An important stage in modern feminism was reached in Kate Millett's *Sexual Politics* (1970). She used the term 'patriarchy' (rule of the father) to describe the cause of women's oppression. Patriarchy subordinates the female to the male or treats the female as an inferior male. Power is exerted directly or indirectly in civil and domestic life, to constrain women. Despite democratic advances, women, argues Millet, have continued to be coerced by a system of sex-role stereotyping to which they are subjected from the earliest age. She borrows from social science the important distinction between 'sex' and 'gender'. Sex is determined biologically, but 'gender' is a psychological concept which refers to *culturally* acquired sexual identity. Margaret Mead, the anthropologist, had shown that in non-Western societies the attributes assigned to men and women can differ widely; men can be peace-loving, women warlike. Millett and other feminists have attacked social scientists who treat the culturally learned 'female' characteristics (passivity, etc.) as natural. She recognises that women as much as men perpetuate these attitudes in women's magazines and family ideology. Sex 'roles' as perpetuated in society are in her view repressive. The acting out of the roles in the unequal relation of domination and subordination is what Millet calls 'sexual politics'.

In the earlier phase of modern feminist writing on literature (Kate Millett, Germaine Greer, Mary Ellmann) the emphasis was often quite political in the sense that the writers were expressing angry feelings of injustice and were engaged in raising women's 'political' awareness of their oppression by men. It is interesting to note the similarities between this type of feminism and other forms of political radicalism. Women as an oppressed group might be and have been compared to blacks and to the working class; although, as Simone de Beauvoir points out, unlike blacks, women are not a minority, and unlike the proletariat, women are not a product of history. It has been said that the most oppressed category of all is black, working-class, *and* female. The arguments of each oppressed group take similar forms: the oppressor is seen as consciously endeavouring to sustain the oppression indefinitely through ideology (racist, bourgeois or patriarchal); each defends its members against misrepresentation and stereotyping in fiction and the media; and each conducts a 'political' struggle to raise consciousness among the oppressed and to effect a radical change in the power relations between oppressor and oppressed. In these crudely political theories ideology is reduced to a completely one-dimensional weapon of domination. For Millett, as Cora Kaplan put it, 'ideology is the universal penile club which men of all classes use to beat women with.' Men simply project on to women attributes of weakness and masochism. This ignores the unconscious psychological processes of gender formation and the more impersonal social and economic motors of women's oppression.

How does this affect literature? First, literary values and conventions have themselves been shaped by men, and women have often struggled to express their own concerns in what may well have been inappropriate forms. In narrative, for example, the shaping conventions of adventure and romantic pursuit have a 'male' impetus and purposiveness. Secondly, the male writer addresses his readers as if they are always men. Advertising provides obvious parallel examples in mass culture. The T.V. advert for an electric shower, which presents a woman who tantalisingly drops her towel just too late for the (male) viewer to glimpse her naked body, blatantly excludes the female viewer. However, it is clear from this example that it is also possible for the female viewer to collude in the exclusion and to view 'as a man'. In the same way the woman reader can be (unconsciously) coerced into reading as a man. In order to resist this indoctrination of the female reader Kate Millett, in *Sexual Politics*, exposes the oppressive representations of sexuality to be found in male fiction. By deliberately foregrounding the view of a *female* reader, she highlights the male domination which pervades the sexual descriptions in the novels of D.H. Lawrence, Henry Miller, Norman Mailer, and Jean Genet. For example, she castigates a passage in Miller's *Sexus* ('I slid to my knees and buried my head in her muff', etc.) and argues that it 'carries the tone ... of one male relating an exploit to another male in the masculine vocabulary with its point of view'. She describes the central acts in Mailer's *The American Dream*, in which Rojack first murders his wife and then sodomises the maid Ruta, as 'a war waged' against women 'in terms of murder and sodomy'. Millett's book provided a powerful critique of patriarchal culture, but some feminists believe that her selection of male authors was too unrepresentative, and others think that she does not sufficiently understand the subversive power of the imagination in fiction. She misses, for example, the deeply deviant nature of Genet's *The Thief's Journal*, and sees, in the homosexual world depicted, only an implied subjection and degradation of the female; the domination and subordination among the gays is regarded as just another version of the oppressive heterosexual pattern. In *The Prisoner of Sex* (1971) Norman Mailer launched an aggressive attack on Millett and often scored points against her failures to allow for the fictional context of particular passages. It appears that, for Millett, male authors are compelled by their gender to reproduce the oppressive sexual politics of the real world in their fiction. This approach would not do justice, for example, to Joyce's treatment of female sexuality. Not only Mailer but also some feminists have seen Millett as holding a one-dimensional view of male domination; she treats sexist ideology as a blanket of oppression which all male writers inevitably promote.

Millett and Shulamith Firestone (*The Dialectic of Sex*, 1972) regard male domination as primary and quite independent of other social and economic forms of oppression. Firestone's theoretical aim is to substitute sex for class as the prime historical determinant. The 'class struggle' is itself a product of the organisation of the biological family unit. Michèle Barrett has argued that the notion of 'patriarchy' as used by Millett and Firestone suggests a universal domination with no historical origins or variations. By ignoring the *articulation* of patriarchy and capitalism, she argues, they oversimplify a complex process. Several elements must be related. They include: the economic organisation of households and its accompanying 'familial ideology'; the division of labour in the economic system; the systems of education and the state; the cultural processes in which men and women are differently represented; and the nature of gender identity and the relationship between sexuality and biological reproduction.

Barrett presents a Marxist feminist analysis of gender representation. First, she applauds Virginia Woolf's materialist argument that the conditions under which men and women *produce* literature are materially different and influence the form and content of what they write. We cannot separate questions of gender stereotyping from their material conditions in history. This means that liberation will not come merely from changes in culture. Secondly, the ideology of gender affects the way the writings of men and women are read and how canons of excellence are established. Thirdly, feminist critics must take account of the *fictional* nature of literary texts and not indulge in 'rampant moralism' by condemning all male authors for all the sexism in their books and approving women authors for raising the issues of gender. Texts have no fixed meanings: interpretations depend on the situation and ideology of the reader. Nevertheless, women can and should try to assert their influence upon the way in which gender is defined and represented culturally.

Women's writing and gynocritics

Elaine Showalter's *A Literature of Their Own* (1977) examines British women novelists since the Brontës from the point of view of women's experience. She takes the view that, while there is no fixed or innate female sexuality or female imagination, there is nevertheless a profound *difference* between women's writing and men's, and that a whole tradition of writing has been neglected by male critics: 'the lost continent of the female tradition has risen like Atlantis from the sea of English Literature.' She divides this tradition into three phases. The first, the 'feminine' phase, 1840–80, includes Elizabeth Gaskell and George Eliot. Women writers imitated and internalised the dominant male aesthetic standards, which required that women writers remain gentlewomen. The main sphere of their work was their immediate domestic and social circle. They suffered guilt about their 'selfish' commitment to authorship and accepted certain limitations in expression, avoiding coarseness and sensuality. However, I would argue that even the somewhat Puritan George Eliot managed to imply a good deal of sensuality in *The Mill on the Floss*. In any case, coarseness and sensuality were not readily acceptable in men's fiction; Hardy's controversial *Tess of the D'Urbervilles* had to resort to implication and poetic imagery to convey the sexuality of the heroine.

The 'feminist' phase, 1880–1920, includes writers such as Elizabeth Robins and Olive Schreiner. The radical feminists of this period advocated separatist Amazonian utopias and suffragette sisterhoods. The third, 'female', phase (1920 onwards) inherited characteristics of the former phases and developed the idea of specifically female writing and female experience. Rebecca West, Katherine Mansfield and Dorothy Richardson were the most important early 'female' novelists in this phase, according to Showalter. In the same period in which Joyce and Proust were writing long novels of subjective consciousness, Richardson's long novel *Pilgrimage* took as its subject female consciousness. Her views on writing anticipate recent feminist theories. She favoured a sort of negative capability, a 'multiple receptivity' which rejects definite views and opinions which she called 'masculine things'. Showalter writes that 'she also rationalized the problem of her "shapeless outpourings" by working out a theory that saw shapelessness as the natural expression of female empathy, and pattern as the sign of male one-sideness.' She consciously tried to produce elliptical and fragmented sentences in order to convey what she considered to be the shape and texture of the female mind. After Virginia Woolf, a new frankness about sexuality (adultery, lesbianism, etc.) enters women's fiction, especially in Jean Rhys. A new generation of university educated women, who no longer felt the need to express feminine discontents, included A.S. Byatt, Margaret Drabble, Christine Brooke-Rose, and Brigid Brophy. However, in the early seventies a shift towards a more angry tone occurs in the novels of Penelope Mortimer, Muriel Spark, and Doris Lessing.

Virginia Woolf wrote a good deal about women's writing and, like Richardson, is an important precursor of modern feminist criticism. While she never adopted a feminist stance, she continually examined the problems facing women writers. She believed that women had always faced social and economic obstacles to their literary ambitions. She herself was conscious of the restricted education she received (she knew no Greek, for example). By adopting the Bloomsbury sexual ethic of 'androgyny', she accepted a serene withdrawal from the struggle between male and female sexuality. Rejecting a feminist consciousness, she hoped to achieve a balance between a 'male' self-realisation and 'female' self-annihilation. Her repeated attacks of madness and eventual suicide suggest that the struggle to transcend sexuality failed. She wanted her femininity to be unconscious so that she might 'escape from the confrontation with femaleness or maleness' (*A Room of One's Own*).

Despite this troublesome commitment to androgyny, she

showed great awareness of the distinctness of women's writing. Her account of the eccentric Duchess of Newcastle wittily draws attention to the very 'feminine' creativity of a seventeenth-century woman writer:

> **though her philosophies are futile, and her plays intolerable, and her verses mainly dull, the vast bulk of the Duchess is leavened by a vein of authentic fire. One cannot help following the lure of her erratic and lovable personality as it meanders and twinkles through page after page. There is something noble and Quixotic and high-spirited, as well as crack-brained and bird-witted, about her.**

Virgina Woolf seems to be saying that the Duchess's dull 'masculine' oeuvre ('vast bulk') is brightened by a playful 'female' waywardness ('erratic', 'meanders'). The last sentence is especially revealing: 'noble and Quixotic' sound like masculine attributes, while 'crack-brained and bird-witted' sound feminine. By combining the contrasting connotations, she reaches towards a sort of androgynous neutrality.

Her most influential and interesting essay about women writers is 'Professions for Women'. She regarded her own career as hindered in two ways. First, as were many nineteenth-century writers, she was imprisoned by the ideology of womanhood. The ideal of 'the Angel in the House' called for women to be sympathetic, unselfish, and pure; to create time and space for writing a woman had to use feminine wiles and flattery. Secondly, the taboo about expresssing female passion prevented her from 'telling the truth about [her] own experiences as a body'. This denial of female sexuality and the unconscious was never overcome in her work or life. Indeed, she did not believe in a female unconscious, but thought that women wrote differently not because they were different psychologically from men but because their social experience was different. Her attempts to write about the experiences of women were conscious and aimed at discovering linguistic ways of describing the confined life of women. She believed that when women finally achieved social and economic equality with men, there would be nothing to prevent women from freely developing their artistic talents.

The early gynocritical text which has most impressed me is Mary Ellmann's *Thinking about Women* (1968). She belongs to the early 'political' phase of modern feminism, but anticipates more subtle developments. She wittily attacks 'phallic criticism', mocking Walter Pater's absurd notion of 'Manliness in art' which he defined as a fully conscious artfulness, a 'tenacity of intuition and purpose, the spirit of construction as opposed to what is literally incoherent or ready to fall to pieces, and in opposition to what is hysteric or works at random'. Unlike Showalter, Ellmann does not tend to identify female writing with female experience, but relates it to certain literary styles. Women writers, she argues, often establish a subversively different perspective by undermining definiteness of judgement and fixity of focus. Ivy Compton-Burnett's novels reduce definite 'points of view' to marginal asides, denying to them the authority of 'masculine' judgements. This type of writing often produces an effect of *comic stasis*, in which judgements are forestalled and conclusions unreached. In her view, not all women writers adopt a female writing style; Mary McCarthy writes with too much authority and Charlotte Brontë with too much commitment and serious passion. Conversely, that subtly undermining stylistic preciosity valued by Ellmann is to be found in Oscar Wilde and, one might add, Joe Orton, both of whom were sexually unorthodox.

Ellmann draws attention to Jane Bowles' *Two Serious Ladies* (1943), a bizarre comic novel about two women who decline into a sub-world of debauchery while retaining a detached propriety of utterance and demeanour. The women celebrate in a completely unselfconscious manner the subtle joys of female independence. The novel is a splendid early exploration of the female subversion of male values. Frieda Copperfield hankers after a comfortable hotel in Panama which she visits with her husband. He prefers to spend money on 'objects' which will last and, when Frieda disagrees, he sulks:

> 'If you are going to be miserable, we'll go to the Hotel Washington,' said Mr. Copperfield. Suddenly he lost his dignity. His eyes clouded over and he pouted. 'But I'll be wretched there, I can assure you. It's going to be so God-damned dull.' He was like a baby and Mrs. Copperfield was obliged to comfort him. He had a trick way of making her feel responsible.

Only a woman novelist could take such wicked revenge on the male's dignity and his 'spirit of construction'! Bowles uses her protagonists to explore a 'female' consciousness and value system. They are attracted to the forbidden because it challenges male authority. They search light-heartedly and irresponsibly for happiness and 'inner peace'. Christina Goering abandons her upper-class respectability and eventually becomes a high-class call-girl in Panama. In the course of her 'decline' she observes the odd defences and contradictions of her male admirers. Arnold's father, who rather blatantly competes with his son's courtship of Christina, suddenly refers to his hopes that she will be 'by my side'. She asks 'What does this involve?' He replies, 'It involves ... your being a true woman. Sympathetic and willing to defend all that I say and do. At the same time prone to scolding me just a little.' Next morning he appears with open collar and rumpled hair, trying to dismiss the responsibilities of marriage with a Bohemian unconcern, and declares, failing to notice his inconsistencies, 'The beauty of the artist lies in the childlike soul.' In her pursuit of 'sainthood', Christina finally asks herself the 'male' question, 'Is it possible that a part of me hidden from my sight is piling sin upon sin as fast as Mrs Copperfield?' The narrator coolly concludes: 'This latter possibility Miss Goering thought to be of considerable interest but of no great importance.'

Two Serious Ladies points towards a feminist criticism which transcends the harsh polemics of Kate Millett and yet subtly undermines all 'male' values and stereotypes. For example, Mrs Copperfield declares 'I've always been a body-worshipper ... but that doesn't mean that I fall in love with people who have beautiful bodies. Some of the bodies I've liked have been awful.' Here what men might regard as female quirkiness is silently translated into instructive female difference.

French feminist critical theory

French feminism has been deeply affected by psychoanalysis, especially by Lacan's reworking of Freud's theories (see chapter 4). French feminists, by following Lacan's theories, have overcome the hostility towards Freud shared by most feminists. Before Lacan, Freud's theories, especially in the United States, had been reduced to a crude biological level: the female child, seeing the male organ, recognises herself as female because she lacks the penis. She defines herself negatively and suffers an inevitable 'penis-envy'. According to Freud, penis-envy is universal in women and is responsible for their 'castration complex', which results in their regarding themselves as '*hommes manqués*' rather than a positive sex in their own right. Ernest Jones was the first to dub Freud's theory 'phallocentric', a term widely adopted by feminists when discussing male domination in general.

Juliet Mitchell, in *Psychoanalysis and Feminism* (1975), defends Freud, arguing that 'psychoanalysis is not a recommendation *for* a patriarchal society but an analysis *of* one'. Freud, she believes, is describing the *mental representation* of a social reality, not reality itself. Her defence of Freud's concept of penis-envy and his notions of sexual difference have been found unconvincing by many feminists. Her rehabilitation of Freud owes something to Lacan but, as Jane Gallop shows, Mitchell fails to engage with Lacan's strategic use of Saussurean linguistics.

Inevitably feminists have reacted bitterly to a view of woman as 'passive, narcissistic, masochistic and penis-envying' (Eagleton), as nothing in her self but only measurable in relation to a male norm. However, some French feminists have emphasised that Freud's 'penis' or 'phallus' is a 'symbolic' concept and not a biological actuality. Lacan's use of the term draws upon the ancient connotations of the phallus in fertility cults. The word is also used in theological and anthropological literature with reference to the organ's symbolic meaning as *power*.

One of Lacan's diagrams has been found useful by feminists in making clear the arbitrariness of sexual roles:

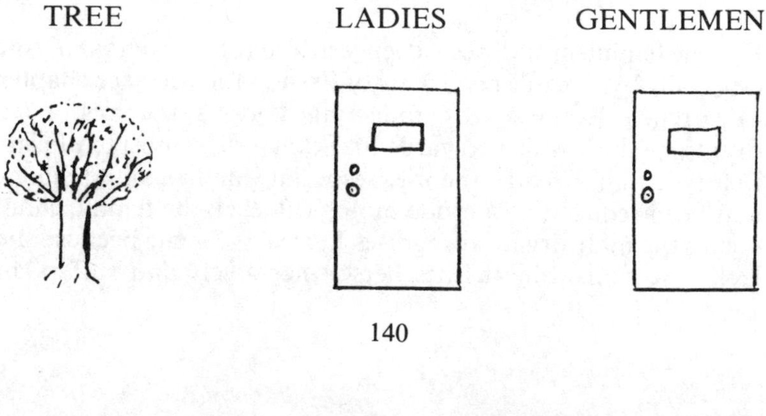

The first sign is 'iconic', and describes the 'natural' correspondence between word and thing. The sign sums up the old pre-Saussurean notion of language, according to which words and things appear naturally unified in a universal meaning. The second diagram destroys the old harmony: the signifiers 'ladies' and 'gentlemen' are attached to identical doors. The 'same' doors are made to enter the differential system of language, so that we are made to see them as 'different'. In the same way 'woman' is a signifier, not a biological female. There is no simple correspondence between a specific body and the signifier 'woman'. However, this does not mean that, if we remove the distorting inscription of the signifier, a 'real', 'natural' woman will come to light as she would have been before the onset of symbolisation. We can never step outside the process of signification on to some neutral ground. Any feminist resistance to phallocentrism (the dominance of the phallus as a signifier) must come from within the signifying process. As we saw in chapter 4, the signifier is more powerful than the 'subject', who 'fades' and suffers 'castration'. 'Woman' represents a subject position banished to outer darkness ('the dark continent') by the castrating power of phallocentrism, and indeed, because such domination works through discourse, by 'phallogocentrism' (domination by phallus logic).

For Lacan the question of phallocentrism is inseparable from the structure of the sign. The signifier, the phallus, holds out the promise of full presence and power, which, because it is unobtainable, threatens both sexes with the 'castration complex'. The complex is structured in exactly the same way as language and the unconscious: the individual subject's entry into language produces a 'splitting' as a result of the subject's sense of loss when the signifiers fail to deliver their promise of a full presence (see chapter 4). Males and females, in different ways, lack the wholeness of sexuality symbolised in the phallus. Social and cultural factors, such as gender stereotypes, may accentuate or diminish the impact of this unconscious 'lack', but the phallus, being a signifer of full presence and not a physical organ, remains a universal source of 'castration complex': the lack which it promises to fill can never be filled. Lacan sometimes calls this insistent signifier 'Name-of-the-Father', thus emphasising its non-'real', non-biological mode of existence. Human beings all organise their relations of love and hate around the question of the phallus's presence or absence. This emphasis on a universal pattern is typically structuralist.

The role of the father is also privileged in the process which leads to the formation of fully gendered individuals. Lacan's account of the Freudian Oedipus Complex describes three phases:

1. The male child identifies completely with the mother, and wishes, unconsciously, to complete everything lacking in her. He therefore identifies with the phallus, the object of his mother's desire, and in doing so presents himself as a mere blank.
2. The father forbids both the child's identification with the phallus and the mother's possible acceptance of this identification. Thus, the child encounters the Law of the Father which threatens him with 'castration'.
3. The child then identifies with the father, as he who 'has' the phallus (no one can actually have it), and forms a sense of his own identity as a being who will one day occupy the place of the father. The child represses his original desire and accepts instead the Law (what Freud calls the 'reality principle').

The child arrives at a sense of identity only by entering the 'symbolic' order of language, which is made up of relations of *similarity* and *difference*. Only by accepting the exclusions (if this, then not that) imposed by the Law of the Father can the child enter the gendered space assigned to it by the linguistic order. It is essential to recognise the *metaphoric* nature of the father's role. He is installed in the position of lawgiver not because he has a superior procreative function (though people have believed this in the past) but merely as an effect of the linguistic system. The mother recognises the speech of the father because she has access to the *signifier* of the paternal function ('Name-of-the-Father'), which regulates desire in a 'civilised' (i.e. repressed) manner. Only by accepting the necessity of sexual difference (either/or) and regulated desire can a child become 'socialised'.

Feminists have sometimes objected that, even if we take a strictly 'symbolic' view of the phallus, the privileged position in signification accorded to it in Lacan's theories is quite disproportionate. According to Jane Gallop, the application of

Lacan's categories to sexual difference seems inevitably to involve a subordination of female sexuality. The man is 'castrated' by not being the total fullness promised by the phallus, while the woman is 'castrated' by not being male. The female's passage through the Oedipus complex is less clear-cut. First, she must transfer her affection from the mother to the father before his Law can forbid incest, and secondly, since she is already 'castrated', it is hard to see what takes the place in her case of *threatened* castration in the male's development. What is there to compel her acceptance of the Law? Nevertheless, the advantage of Lacan's approach is that it gets away from biological determinism and puts Freudian psychoanalysis in touch with the social system (through language).

As Jane Gallop has noted, Lacan tends to promote a 'feminist' anti-logocentric discourse. Though not consciously feminist, he is 'coquettish', playful, and 'poetic', refusing to assert conclusions, or to establish truths. When he recalls Freud's unanswered question 'What does Woman want?' (*Was will das Weib?*), he concludes that the question must remain open since the female is 'fluid', and fluidity is 'unstable'. 'Woman never speaks *pareil* [similar, equal, like]. What she emits is flowing [*fluent*]. Cheating [*Flouant*].' There is here a danger, once again, of slipping back into a phallocentric system which relegates women to the margin, dismissing them as unstable, unpredictable and fickle. What appears to prevent such a recuperation of female 'openness' to the patriarchal system is the positive *privileging* of this openness. Female sexuality is directly associated with poetic productivity—with the psychosomatic drives which disrupt the tyranny of unitary meaning and logocentric (and therefore phallogocentric) discourse. The major theorists of this view are Julia Kristeva and Hélène Cixous.

Kristeva's work has frequently taken as its central concept a polarity between 'closed' rational systems and 'open' disruptive 'irrational' systems. She has considered poetry to be the 'privileged site' of analysis, because it is poised between the two types of system; and because at certain times poetry has opened itself to the basic impulses of desire and fear which operate outside the 'rational' systems. We have already discussed (chapter 4) her important distinction between the 'semiotic' and the 'symbolic', which is the mother of many other polarities. In avant-garde literature, the primary processes (as described in Lacan's version of Freud's theory of dreams) invade the rational ordering of language and threaten to disrupt the unified subjectivity of the 'speaker' and the reader. The 'subject' is no longer seen as the source of meaning but as the site of meaning, and may therefore undergo a radical 'dispersal' of identity and loss of coherence. The 'drives' experienced by the child in the pre-Oedipal phase are like a language but not yet ordered into one. For this 'semiotic' material to become 'symbolic' it must be stabilised, and this involves repression of the flowing and rhythmic drives. The utterance which most approximates to a semiotic discourse is the pre-Oedipal 'babble' of the child. However, language itself retains some of this semiotic flux and the poet is especially attuned to tapping its resonances. Because the psychosomatic drives are pre-Oedipal they are associated with the body of the mother; the free-floating sea of the womb and the enveloping sensuousness of the mother's breast are the first places of pre-Oedipal experience. The 'semiotic' is thus inevitably associated with the female body, while the 'symbolic' is linked with the Law of the Father which censors and represses in order that discourse may come into being. Woman is the silence of the 'unconscious' which precedes discourse. She is the 'Other', which stands outside and threatens to disrupt the conscious (rational) order of speech. On the other hand, since the pre-Oedipal phase is undifferentiated sexually, the semiotic is not unequivocally feminine. One might say that Kristeva stakes a claim on behalf of women to this unrepressed and unrepressive flow of liberating energy. The avant-garde poet, man or woman, enters the Body-of-the-Mother and resists the Name-of-the-Father. Mallarmé, for example, by subverting the laws of syntax, subverts the Law of the Father, and identifies with the mother through his recovery of the 'maternal' semiotic flux. Kristeva sees this poetic revolution as closely linked with political revolution in general and feminist liberation in particular: the feminist movement must invent a 'form of anarchism' which will correspond to the 'discourse of the avant-garde'. Anarchism is inevitably the philosophical and political position adopted by a feminism determined to destroy the dominance of phallogocentrism.

A number of French feminists (including Chantal Chawaf, Xavière Gauthier, and Luce Irigaray) have argued that female sexuality is a subterranean and unknown entity. Hélène Cixous' essay, 'The Laugh of the Medusa' is a celebrated manifesto of women's writing which calls for women to put their 'bodies' into their writing. While Virginia Woolf abandoned the struggle to speak of the female body, Cixous writes ecstatically of the teeming female unconscious: 'Write yourself. Your body must be heard. Only then will the immense resources of the unconscious spring forth.' There is no universal female mind; on the contrary the female imagination is infinite and beautiful. The truly liberated woman writer, when she exists, will say

> I ... overflow; my desires have invented new desires, my body knows unheard-of songs. Time and again ... I have felt so full of luminous torrents that I could burst—burst with forms much more beautiful than those which are put up in frames and sold for a stinking fortune.

Since writing is the place where subversive thought can germinate, it is especially shameful that the phallocentric tradition has, for the most part, succeeded in not giving women their say. Woman must uncensor herself, recover 'her goods, her organs, her immense bodily territories which have been kept under seal'. She must throw off her guilt (for being too hot or too frigid, too motherly or too unmaternal, etc.). The heart of Cixous' theory is her rejection of theory: feminist writing 'will always surpass the discourse that regulates the phallocentric system'.

Cixous opposes the sort of neutral bisexuality espoused by Virginia Woolf, and advocates instead what she calls 'the *other bisexuality*' which refuses to 'annul differences but stirs them up'. Barthes' study of *Sarrasine* (see chapter 4) is a perfect example of narrative bisexuality. Indeed Cixous' account of female sexuality often reminds one of Barthes' description of the avant-garde text. 'A woman's body,' writes Cixous, 'with its thousand and one thresholds of ardor ... will make the old single-grooved mother tongue reverberate with more than one language.' She is talking about '*jouissance*', which, in Barthes and Kristeva, combines connotations of sexual orgasm and polysemic speech; the pleasure of the text, abolishing all repressions, reaches an intense crisis (the death of meaning). This transgression of the laws of phallocentric discourse is the woman writer's special task. Having always operated 'within' male-dominated discourse, the woman needs 'to invent for herself a language to get inside of'.

Cixous' approach is visionary, imagining a possible language rather than describing an existing one. It runs the risk run by other approaches, already discussed, of driving women into an obscure unconscious retreat where silence reigns interrupted only by uterine 'babble'. This danger is well understood by Kristeva, who sees women writers, rather in the way that Virginia Woolf saw them, as caught between the father and the mother. On the one hand, as writers they inevitably collude with 'phallic dominance, associated with the privileged father-daughter relationship, which gives rise to the tendency towards mastery, science, philosophy, professorships, etc ...'. On the other hand, 'we flee everything considered 'phallic' to find refuge in the valorisation of a silent underwater body, thus abdicating any entry into history'.

Our sketch of feminism and feminist literary theory has, I hope, suggested the range and variety of approaches which have evolved in recent years. It has proved difficult for feminists to develop theories without resort to male theorists. Several women have argued that an adequate feminist theory can arise only from within women's experience or from their unconscious; women must produce their own language, and their own conceptual universe, which may not appear rational to men. However, Hélène Cixous, who is the prophet of the female Word, draws significantly upon the theories of Barthes and Lacan. Whatever the difficulties, women have the right to assert their own values, to explore their own consciousness, and to develop new forms of expression corresponding to their values and consciousness. The literary canons of the past must inevitably be revalued and reshaped, as the balance of power shifts among men and women critics and as the question of gender becomes more prominent in theoretical debates. Gender criticism will never be able to resort to a universally accepted body of theory. In a recent book, Terry Eagleton argues that the women's movement has succeeded in developing the most honest and challenging unification of political and cultural action. All critical theory is 'political' in the sense that it always seeks to control discourse. Feminists are quite consciously trying to wrest their share of discursive power from men. Whatever theoretical strategies serve this end are grist to their mill. For this reason feminist critical theory is a microcosm of the entire theoretical universe, in which a power struggle continues unabated.

Selected Reading

Basic Texts

Abel, Elizabeth (ed.), *Writing and Sexual Difference* (Harvester Press, Brighton, 1982), originally in *Critical Inquiry*.

Cixous, Hélène, 'The laugh of the Medusa', *Signs*, 1(1976), 875–93.

de Beauvoir, Simone, *The Second Sex*, trans. H.M. Parshley (Bantam Books, New York, 1949, 1961; Penguin, Harmondsworth, 1974).

Donovan, Josephine (ed.), *Feminist Literary Criticism: Explorations in Theory* (Kentucky University Press, Lexington, 1975).

Ellmann, Mary, *Thinking about Women* (Harcourt Brace, 1968; Virago, London, 1979).

Jacobus, Mary, ed., *Women Writing and Writing about Women* (Croom Helm, London, and Barnes & Noble, New York, 1979).

Marks, Elaine and de Courtivron, Isabelle, (eds), *New French Feminisms: An Anthology* (Harvester Press, Brighton, 1981).

Showalter, Elaine, *A Literature of Their Own: British Women Novelists from Brontë to Lessing* (Princeton University Press, 1977; Virago, London, 1978).

Woolf, Virginia *Women and Writing*, intro. M. Barrett (Women's Press, London, 1979). Anthology.

General Background on Feminism

Barrett, Michèle, *Women's Oppression Today: Problems in Marxist Feminist Analysis* (Verso Editions, London, 1980).

Eisenstein, Hester, *Contemporary Feminist Thought* (Unwin, London and Sydney, 1984).

Firestone, Shulamith, *The Dialectic of Sex* (Women's Press, London, 1979).

Gallop, Jane, *Feminism and Psychoanalysis: The Daughter's Seduction* (Macmillan, London and Basingstoke, 1982).

Millet, Kate, *Sexual Politics* (Virago, London, 1977).

Mitchell, Juliet, *Psychoanalysis and Feminism* (Penguin, Harmondsworth, 1975).

Rich, Adrienne, *On Lies, Secrets, and Silence: Selected Prose 1966–1978* (Virago, London, 1980).

Secondary Reading in Criticism

Culler, Jonathan, 'Reading as a woman', in *On Deconstruction: Theory and Criticism after Structuralism* (Routledge & Kegan Paul, London, Melbourne and Henley, 1983).

Fetterly, Judith, *The Resisting Reader: A Feminist Approach to American Fiction* (Indiana University Press, 1978).

McConnell-Ginet, S., Borker, R., and Furman, N. (eds), *Women and Language in Literature and Society* (Praeger, New York, 1980).

Ruthven, K.K., *Feminist Literary Studies: an Introduction* (Cambridge University Press, Cambridge, 1984).

Journals: *Feminist Review, m/f* and *Signs*, publish important work. *Diacritics* (Winter, 1975) was a special issue: 'Textual politics: feminist criticism'.

INDEX

Critical Theory Since 1965
ed. by Hazard Adams & Leroy Searle